Asian Encounters

EARLY LIFE, TRAVELS, AND FAMILY

Asian Encounters

EARLY LIFE, TRAVELS, AND FAMILY

by

MILLIDGE P. WALKER III

Contents

Preface

I WOULD SAY PROBABLY FROM AROUND 2003 TO 2005, around the time we moved into The Mirabella, I began to lose my memory and I felt that I didn't have enough memory to proceed with my memoirs. I really didn't do anything about continuing them except to include an account of our trip through Africa. That was because Irene had written a book about it, so I was able to read the book to refresh my memory. Because I found that my memory was failing me, I got Irene to help me with all of the events. She helps me with my memory and we exchange comments to refresh each other's memory. From then on until the end of the book, it is really a memoir of the two of us, not just me.

CHAPTER ONE

Origins in Shanghai

THE FAMILY

 AM THE YOUNGEST OF FOUR CHILDREN OF MILLIDGE Penderell and Eleanor Landis Walker. My father, from whom I inherited the name, had been educated as a mechanical engineer. After having spent brief periods working for a yacht builder and a bicycle company and even the Stanley Steamer automobile company, all in Connecticut, he joined the missionary service of the Episcopal church and was sent in 1902 to Shanghai as a professor of math and basic engineering at St. John's University. He came from a long line of staunch Anglicans, and his father was a clergyman of that denomination.

My mother, the daughter of a Presbyterian missionary in Japan, met my father on the tennis courts in Karuizawa, a favorite mountain resort for expatriates living in the Tokyo area. At that time my father had been living in Shanghai for about ten years and had tried to get out of the city each summer so as to avoid the most abysmal weather: very hot and humid with frequent thunderstorms. I heard rumors on the St. John's campus that he had courted the Episcopal bishop's elder daughter, who rebuffed him, thank goodness, as my recollection of her was as a rather stern, unbending woman with no sense of humor.

An amusing footnote to this encounter in Karuizawa occurred seventy-six years later when my mother was living in a retirement home in Washington and was visited by the then crown prince and later emperor (1989–2019) of Japan, Akihito, who happened to be in the United States on a state visit. My mother remarked that like the prince and his bride-to-be, she had met her spouse on the tennis courts of Karuizawa. This obviously amused the prince and they exchanged reminiscences of Japan. Not long after she received a signed photograph of the prince and his spouse.

My maternal grandfather, Henry Moor Landis, arrived in Japan shortly after Admiral Peary and his "black fleet" appeared in Tokyo Bay and before the Meiji restoration, when the Tokugawa rulers were overthrown and the Emperor was once again elevated to his rightful imperial position. A minister of the Presbyterian church, Henry Landis founded a boys' school that became known as the Meiji Gakuin, and in later years became a liberal arts college. He came from a Pennsylvania Dutch family, graduated from Princeton, where he attended the theological seminary, and did postgraduate studies at the University of Berlin. He must have been there when the university was the seat of German idealistic philosophy with scholars such as von Ranke and Treitschke holding forth.

My grandmother came from Dresden, Saxony, and moved to the United States to work as a nanny in a Bucks County household. Their paths crossed in the States, and as they had something in common as they both spoke German. I often heard of my grandfather's good works, but he died the year I was born. He took a great interest in the design and construction of his school, but at one point he fell from the scaffolding of a building and died after lying in a coma for several months. This took place around the time of the great Tokyo earthquake of 1923, which practically leveled the entire city. My grandmother stayed on in Tokyo for another twelve years; she was much beloved by female members of the aristocracy as a teacher of German. As she grew older and more frail, she came to live with us in Shanghai. At that time she tried to teach me German, but as she was by then bedridden, I could easily avoid her good intentions.

My mother, the oldest of five children, was homeschooled until she was about sixteen; in which language, English or German, I'm not sure. She was bilingual, and spent much of her life after she married my father and moved to Shanghai teaching German to Chinese students. I am sure she and her four siblings were homeschooled, but the two boys and the youngest girl all attended college in the States and had professions: engineer, lawyer, and pediatrician respectively. As the oldest, she was sent along with her younger sister, Paula, to a music conservatory in Dresden and became proficient in both violin and viola, while Paula studied piano. She used to tell us stories about the many proposals of marriage she received on the lengthy voyage back to the Orient. Many single men were going out there to work and there were few women where they were going. One young man was persuasive and he accompanied her to Tokyo, but her father rebuffed him, claiming that she was too young and he knew nothing about his background. On her return to Tokyo, she was involved in giving violin lessons to the children of the aristocratic families who were friends of her mother's. While her younger siblings went to the United States to pursue their education, my mother stayed on in Japan teaching music and spending summers in Karuizawa, a resort in the mountains of Honshu. The summers in Tokyo are miserably hot and humid, and Karuizawa is the choice of Tokyo expatriates.

The summer of 1912 was particularly significant for her. She enjoyed playing tennis and at one point was asked to partner with a man from Shanghai in a mixed doubles match. They won the match and others that summer, and before the partner left to return to Shanghai, he proposed, and on this occasion she accepted. He had a full teaching load and could not return to Tokyo before the Christmas break; they were married on the 2nd of December and the couple lived together for the next thirty-nine years at No. 9 St John's University and produced five children. I was number five, conceived as a replacement for an older male twin, Millidge Penderell Walker, Jr., who died at two years of age. To keep the pretentious name active, I was named III.

I remember my mother during the Shanghai days as being very busy, for besides teaching German, she trained the choir at the campus church, played the organ at most services, and joined a string quartet. This was in addition to running a household of a husband, four children, and four servants. My parents had a fairly lively social life, and having four live-in servants provided them with all the mobility they needed. After about twelve years of teaching mathematics, my father became treasurer and general manager of all Episcopal and Anglican missionary activities in China and the Philippines, which meant that he traveled a good deal; since travel in those days was by slow train, houseboat, or wheelbarrow, his absences were fairly long. However, during my childhood, roads had been built, at least in the Yangtze delta, the rail lines had been extended from Nanjing to Beijing, and there was even air service between the major cities.

My father's ancestry was no less interesting despite being very English. The Penderell descendants to this day receive a pension from the English crown for having hidden King

Charles I from the Roundheads after the battle of Wooster by concealing him in an oak tree. Apparently one group of the Penderells were early settlers of the Maritime Provinces of Canada. The Millidges came to the New World with Lord Oglethorpe, who founded the colony of Georgia. I recently asked a high school classmate who lives in Atlanta to check the state archives to see what she could find about the Millidges. Some months later I received a photocopy of an entry that identified one John Milledge as the first colonial governor of Georgia, who established the state capital at Milledgeville. That distinction lasted only thirty years when the capital was moved to Atlanta, which was on the railway line and commercially more important. But Milledgeville still exists and among other notable features is the home of the state penitentiary. On googling one finds references to both Millidges and Milledges with some overlap, so I assume they are all part of an extended family system.

Incidentally the Millidges must have been a fairly large family. My ancestral branch stayed loyal to the king during the Revolution and were forced to leave the new nation for Canada, taking up residence first in Nova Scotia and then in New Brunswick. This branch of the family seems to have descended from Thomas Millidge, an officer in the colonial army living in New Jersey. He fought with the king's forces and with their defeat fled to Nova Scotia. Would you believe, there is a suburb of Saint John, New Brunswick, named Millidgeville? If one searches the internet for Millidge rather than Milledge, the move to Canada is mentioned and my grandfather identified as having been born in Millidgeville.

It was my paternal grandfather who finally returned to the United States as an Anglican vicar. One of my uncles is an Episcopalian clergyman who was the headmaster of the Meadowbrook School for Boys in a suburb of Philadelphia, and an aunt married a cleric who became the dean of the

Anglican cathedral in Quebec. My favorite uncle graduated from the agricultural school at Cornell and I remember him as a chicken farmer outside of Cape May, New Jersey. He remained a bachelor until he was in his sixties, when he and his girlfriend, a teacher in the Cape May schools, slipped away to Elkton, Maryland, a town known for speedy marriages, and they produced two children, a boy and a girl, of the same age as their cousins' children. He later moved to New England, first in western Massachusetts and then in Connecticut, and worked as contractor and real estate agent. At one point I helped him build a tennis court.

The pattern is very country English, and that was the culture of the Walker family. I found the name Millidge a great burden, being strange, and among the Chinese, difficult to pronounce. Apparently my father was determined to see that the name was passed on to succeeding generations. I must add that it did not get beyond me. I was given the nickname Didi, which means "little brother" in Chinese, which was OK as long as I stayed in China, where there were millions of Didis, but difficult to explain once I came to the States prepared to enter college. My siblings, Mary, Henry, and Elizabeth, had normal names, but the class and history attached to a name like Millidge was lost on me.

SIBLINGS

Apparently in those days it was usual for children to be born in their mother's home, and all five of us were born at No. 9 St John's University. I learned that the procedure was well supervised by a medical doctor and several nurses were in attendance at all times.

It is not easy to categorize my siblings, as each chose different paths toward adulthood and to professions. Mary, the oldest and eight years my senior, and Betty, three years older than I, were very bright students and completed their pre-college education at the Shanghai American School well ahead of their peers and entered elite colleges in the States, Mary at Vassar and Betty at Swarthmore. I recall them as being very athletic in basketball and hockey, which were the chief women's sports at the time. Mary even played with a community team, one of whose members was the coach of the girls' high school team. They were also very accomplished swimmers.

Mary's major in college was biochemistry and as I recall, she worked in a biomedical lab in Boston for Uncle Stephen Maddox, Charlotte Landis's husband and a somewhat uncouth womanizer, until she quit when he tried to become overly intimate. She moved to Washington with a government job where she met Telford Taylor, through Uncle Jim Landis, who was a professor at the Harvard Law School. Jim moved in and out of the Franklin Roosevelt administration and I am unsure where he was located in 1937. Mary and Telford were married a few weeks before my parents and I were due to arrive in the United States on furlough and did not think to wait until we could attend. My father never really forgave Mary for this oversight until five years later when she bore his first grandchild. Telford's specialty was communications law, and he worked as counsel for the newly created Federal Communications Commission. During World War II he was commissioned as a colonel and eventually promoted to Brigadier General when he headed the U.S. prosecution of German war criminals at Nuremberg. Mary and Telford had three children, two girls and a boy. The girls, somewhat older, were left with my parents, who by this time had acquired a home in Sheffield, Massachusetts, while the children's parents were in Germany. The boy was born after the trials were concluded.

In 1932, while the family was traveling around the world

on my father's furlough, my brother Henry was left behind in America, the beneficiary of Uncle William's offer to have him educated at a proper American boys' prep school.

In the summer of 1939, and I get a bit confused with the chronology at this point, my parents decided to summer in Nojiri, a resort in the mountains of Honshu with a lake to which the Tokyo expats retreated when they preferred sailing on the lake to the tennis of Karuizawa. I had hoped to crew on one of the "dog boats," an oversized cat boat, but instead manned the chase boat, a rowboat equipped with an outboard motor, which put out the buoys around which the boats raced and picked up any sailors who fell overboard or were victims of capsizing. That same summer Betty came out to the Far East and joined us in Nojiri and late in the summer returned to Shanghai when we did. She had completed her junior year at Swarthmore and was scheduled to return for the fall semester. She became romantically involved with Ray Burnes, a popular teacher of history at the Shanghai American School and certainly one of my favorites. She was to leave Shanghai on a Canadian steamship to Vancouver; on the day she boarded, war was declared by Britain on Nazi Germany. The departure was delayed at the request of the Admiralty in London while the future disposition of the ship was decided. Betty was on the ship leaning on the rail yelling her goodbyes to her family and boyfriend on the dock below. My parents and I left after about an hour, leaving Ray behind, who sat in a stationary rickshaw he had rented and that had a canvas top to provide shade for passengers. The rickshaw puller was ecstatic for getting paid without having to pull the vehicle. Eventually Ray was able to talk Betty into requesting permission to leave the ship—I don't know if she got her fare back—and marry him. The wedding took place in the church on the St. John's campus; I was an usher. The couple remained in Shanghai for another year, as Ray was made principal of the school, which entitled him to an on-campus apartment. Ray took leave to get a MA at Columbia University Teachers College while Betty completed her BA at Barnard.

By the time they finished their studies, Pearl Harbor had occurred and they never got back to China. Completing their respective degrees, they joined the faculty of the Berkshire School for Boys. By this time Betty was on the verge of producing twin boys, and our parents moved to the campus and were given housing while my father, a former math teacher and engineer, taught a group of Army Air Corps inductees. A couple of years after Pearl Harbor, Ray was drafted and assigned to military intelligence, and the family moved to Washington. My parents soon followed. By this time Mary and Telford had bought a small ranchette with a barn and a paddock in North Chevy Chase that was large enough to accommodate my father and mother, the former doing rehabilitation work on wounded GIs at Walter Reed.

Henry's experience was different. He was five years my senior, and during our furlough of 1932, he had been left behind in the States to finish his schooling at The Lenox School in Massachusetts. I remember very little of his career there, except that the tuition was partially paid by my father's rich brother, who made his fortune importing licorice from the Levant. I also heard that he was a prodigious eater, having won the school egg-eating contest, and that he was called "famine" because there had not been one in China since he left.

Upon graduation from prep school, he earned a degree in mechanical engineering from Stevens Institute of Technology in Hoboken, New Jersey. He was offered a job with the Shanghai Power Company, which was American owned, and returned to China after an absence of eight years. He remained with the company when Pearl Harbor was bombed and was interned by the Japanese for most of four years. He said that he was not mistreated by his captors, but had very little to eat, except an occasional care package from his Russian girlfriend, who fortunately was not interned. But he claimed that he lost ninety pounds, and on his release and his return to the States, he looked very trim with his newly married Russian wife on his arm. He joined a utilities company in Poughkeepsie, New York, where he remained for the rest of his career. His wife Yelena was appointed to the faculty of the foreign language department of Vassar College as a Russian instructor. The family thinks he married her out of guilt not attachment; he played around in the States, then divorced her; he did not remarry.

SHANGHAI: A COLONIAL CITY OF SORTS

Now that you know something about my siblings, I need to go back and fill in some of the gaps. I was told that the usual practice was to give birth to children in the mother's home, and although this was not uniformly done on the St. John's campus, my older siblings and I were born at No. 9 St. John's University. I was born on the eightieth anniversary of the first British occupation of Shanghai, which took place on the 19th of June 1842. Growing up in Shanghai was a unique experience, as it was neither the Occident nor the Orient. Shanghai had a rather singular blend of both: not really a colony in the true sense of the word but administered as though it was. Although the majority of the inhabitants were Chinese, they had no role in the governance of the municipality.

SHANGHAI OF THE 30s

It is interesting that Shanghai is spelled and pronounced the same way as it was during the period of Euro-American-Japanese ascendency. Other major cities in contemporary China, with the other exception being Hong Kong (which should be Anglicized as Hsiang Jiang, translated as fragrant or odorous harbor), are spelled and pronounced in the post-1949 style. Peking is now Beijing, Nanking is now Nanjing (northern and southern capitals respectively), Canton is now Guangzhou, Sian is now Xian, Chungking is now Chongqing. In the local dialect Shanghai was pronounced "Zonghey." I have no idea whether that was the accepted anglicization, as the dialect was considered a language of the streets and not a literary language.

Shanghai was one of the "treaty ports" surrendered by the Imperial Chinese government after several military defeats during the nineteenth century. As a "port," its location is awkward: twelve miles up the Hwang Poo river from where it empties into the Yangtze near that great river's mouth. The site was chosen because it was far enough from the coast to make attack by pirates difficult. Modern ships, particularly large container ships and tankers, have difficulty navigating the muddy river that is congested with smaller craft; docking is limited and midstream mooring adds to traffic problems. The original waterfront is impressive with formidable imperial structures that reflected the European presence: Hong Kong and Shanghai Bank, North China Daily News, the Customs House, the British Consulate, the Cathay and Palace Hotels, and the Shanghai Club, just to name those of the International Settlement; the French Concession had its own set of imposing buildings along the Bund. At right angles away from the Bund was Nangking Road, which was the principal shopping strip for the city. The major department stores, Sincere, Wing On, and the Sun Company, were located along this street, as well as book shops, clothing and textile stores, and best of all the chocolate shop. Nangking Road ended at Tibet Road and became Bubbling Well Road at the Race Course, a large open tract with a race track surrounding a polo and soccer field and drill grounds for police, the Shanghai Volunteer Corps (SVC), and various foreign military units designed to protect the expatriate interests against "native uprisings."

The SVC was somewhat similar to a National Guard unit in the States. Volunteers came from a number of the resident expatriate communities and particularly from the "White Russian" residents. White Russians were those exiles who had fled the Bolshevik Revolution and drifted down to Shanghai from eastern Siberia through Manchuria. This Russian population was fairly large and well established, particularly in the restaurant and nightclub enterprises. Quite a number were employed as senior secretaries in expatriate businesses, some in professions such as public works and utilities, and many were recruited into the police force as officers and upper level sergeants, but these professions did require a working knowledge of English or French. Ordinary constables and traffic cops were largely and conspicuously Sikhs from India in the International Settlement and Montagnards from the Tonkin region of Indo-China in the French Concession. Chinese as police were considered not tough enough, particularly on their compatriots, to ensure enforcement although they did direct traffic. The function of the SVC was somewhat vague. It dated from the early days of the International Settlement and was considered to be Shanghai's "army" as opposed to the military units from Japan, Europe, and the United States.

To the west of the race course and along Bubbling Well Road were some of Shanghai's largest mansions, the homes of longtime resident families such as Sassoon and Kadoorie, who originated in the Middle East. The street was a wide, well-kept, tree-lined street, and these estates were fronted by high brick walls with guarded wrought iron gates. There were other institutions along Bubbling Well Road: the Shanghai

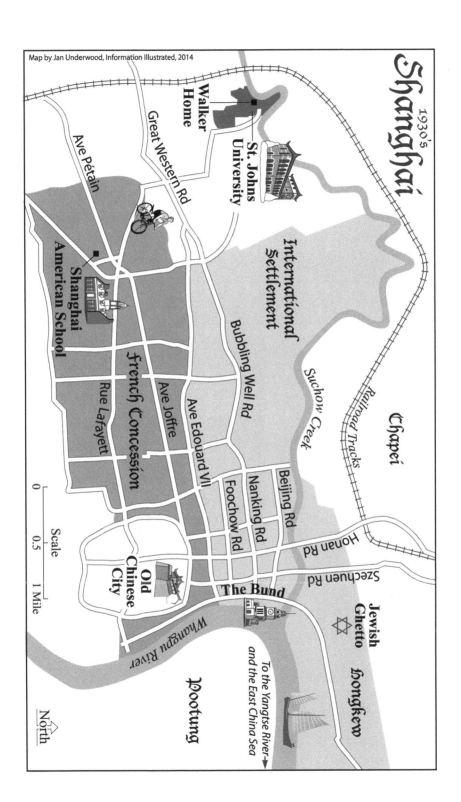

Map by Jan Underwood, Information Illustrated, 2014

Shanghai
1930's

Walker Home

St. Johns University

Great Western Rd

Ave Pétain

Shanghai American School

French Concession

Rue Lafayett

Ave Joffre

Ave Edouard VII

Bubbling Well Rd

International Settlement

Suchow Creek

Railroad Tracks

Chapei

Beijing Rd

Nanking Rd

Foochow Rd

Honan Rd

Szechuen Rd

Old Chinese City

The Bund

Whangpu River

Jewish Ghetto

Hongkew

To the Yangtse River and the East China Sea

Pootung

Scale

0   0.5   1 Mile

North

Public and Thomas Hanbury School, principally for students from British families, the American Woman's Club, and the American cemetery. Bubbling Well, a stinking hole in the sidewalk, marked the official western extremity of the International Settlement; the foreign residential areas continued for another one and a half miles further west, bounded by the railway to Hangzhou on the west and the Suzhou Creek on the north. This extension, although not officially part of the Settlement, was patrolled by Settlement police and its perimeters protected by foreign troops.

Shanghai consisted of two political entities: the "international settlement" and the "French concession." There was an old walled city, the original Shanghai that existed before the "yang kwei-tze" or foreign devils arrived, and then in the 1920s and '30s, the "Greater Shanghai Municipality," which surrounded the foreign territories, came into existence.

The International Settlement was governed by the Municipal Council, which consisted of representatives of the major foreign communities residing in the settlement: five British, three Americans, three Japanese, and several others from Italian, German, and Portuguese communities. Notably unrepresented were Chinese, and if the Chinese had a governance of any kind, it worked through the underworld. The members of the Municipal Council were elected by "rate payers," which restricted the vote to those representing foreign businesses and other institutions such as missionary schools and hospitals. The French Concession was governed directly from Paris and had no self-governing institutions in Shanghai. I remember that the streets were named after British and French colonial heroes or place names, e.g., Avenue Petain, where the American school was located, and Jessfield Road, where we lived. So although China was not officially colonized, Shanghai was definitely a product of the age of imperialism.

Shanghai was a city of great contrasts, not only ethnically and racially, but in terms of class and wealth. Expatriates and Chinese had as little as possible to do with each other, and for the most part different nationalities had little to do with each other, each having its own schools, social clubs, and even places of worship. Missionaries were a bit different since their calling was to convert Chinese to Christianity through "good works": education, health care, and social services such as orphanages. In rare instances they set up small enterprises with Chinese knitting, textiles, and pottery making, which were purchased by other expatriates. "Up country" was quite different because foreigners there had no choice but to deal with Chinese both professionally and socially, as there were too few to form a community of fellow expatriates.

A variety of books have been written about Shanghai, the sin city, the city of decadence, for this would attract readership. Opium dens and brothels were plentiful, and many of these were operated by the Chinese criminal gangs. The most notorious of these was the Green Gang, whose boss was Du Yue-sheng, whose name evoked fear among wealthy Chinese, as they were often the victims of kidnapping by these gangsters. In my senior year of high school, I had a somewhat scary encounter with the Green Gang. One night a couple of male classmates and I spent some time at the Shanghai Gardens, a nightclub with taxi dancers across Jessfield Park from the St. John's campus. Summoning up some bravado, I approached a dancer and suggested we dance. Before I even touched her, the hand of a rather menacing man clenched my arm and pulled me away from the girl. Needless, the three of us understood we were not particularly welcome, and on the way out, I was told that that particular girl was Du's favorite.

Most foreigners spoke little or no Chinese, and if they did, it was mostly the Shanghai dialect and not the proper Mandarin, the Peking version. Very few had studied Chinese, and the few that did were missionaries who worked up country. I spoke with some fluency a brand of the Shanghai dialect that I picked up of the street, laced with slang and profanity. According to my mother, I was denied admission to the living room when my parents were entertaining Chinese friends for fear of what I might utter, not knowing the meaning of the words I had picked up.

The climate of Shanghai is not particularly inviting. It is pretty damp and humid for most of the year, and the summers are particularly bad. Air conditioning did not exist and homes and offices were built with high ceilings and many windows to allow for cross ventilation. This meant that they were hard to heat in the winter, and our home had an iron pot-bellied stove in each of the principal rooms on the ground floor with a pipe running up through the ceiling to heat a bedroom on the floor above. The stove pipe was surrounded by a fat drum that was designed by my father to amplify the heat. My recollection is that we were always too cold in winter and too hot in summer and there was little in between. There must have been some decent weather; I remember the tennis teas that my mother used to give and these were outdoors under a large tree that we kids used to enjoy climbing. The St. John's campus was equipped with four excellent grass courts for use by the faculty; the students had access to two clay courts. The campus gardeners paid exquisite attention to the grass, while the students were expected to maintain their own. This was the way things were in Shanghai, and in those days of western imperialism, even the Chinese faculty did not object. That was to come later; this was still the mid-1930s.

UNIVERSITY LIFE

My father, an engineer by training, put his hand to

architecture and designed a number of academic buildings and faculty homes, including the one we lived in. It was a spacious house with large bedrooms with attached baths. The house had very large porches on both the first and second floors. The lower porch was screened and a wonderful place for dining and socializing during the warm months. One of my delights was to capture butterflies, of which there were many of several varieties, and release them in the enclosed porch. My mother disapproved and had the servants try to shoo them out again. The upstairs porch was for year-round sleeping for the entire family, regardless of the weather. For most of the year one side of the porch was enclosed by bamboo shades, which did a good job of shielding us from the rain. Snow was a very unusual occurrence, although the combination of slightly higher than freezing temperatures and the constant dampness made the weather seem a lot colder than the thermometer indicated. My father designed sleeping bags for each of us that did a good job of keeping us warm and comfortable.

Our house was located about fifty feet from the Soochow Creek, as it was known then. This was the main route from Shanghai to Suzhou, where it joined the Grand Canal, which took tribute from the Emperor's vassals from Hangzhou to Beijing. There was much traffic on the creek, and from our front porch it was a delight to see what was passing. Most vessels were small and hand powered, but every so often a steam launch belching black smoke passed by towing a string of four or five barges. One of my brother's pet projects was to build a rowboat for use on the creek, and my one recollection of an outing was stepping on an errant nail and having to endure the effects of receiving a tetanus shot, which in those days knocked you out for almost a week.

Although the salary of a missionary was pretty meager, we lived very well. Many of our routine expenses were included, such as the house, which was rent free, my father's car, which he had purchased in the States and had shipped to Shanghai at no expense to him, free comprehensive health care at mission hospitals, and financial assistance for children's education. More important were the four servants, whose salaries were possibly subsidized by the mission: a "boy" who waited table and served as the head servant and who supervised the purchase of groceries, charcoal, and coal for the kitchen and in winter for the stoves and fireplaces in the rest of the house. Then the amah (nursemaid), the most important person in the lives of us children. Since I was the youngest, I got her most frequent attention. There were several years when I was considered fragile, skinny, and underweight. I was made to take liquid cod liver oil and later on halibut liver oil, which I thought to be even more vile tasting and which was to be administered to me, since I could not be relied upon to take it on my own. This was the job assigned to the amah, who incidentally had bound feet, which slowed her mobility considerably, enabling me to elude her with no difficulty. Nevertheless, she persisted and used to follow me around the house and out onto the campus shouting, "Didi chuh doong pei," which translates "Didi, take your coin." The reason she called it coin was that the brand of evil-tasting stuff had won a medal in some competition and a likeness of the medal appeared on the label.

In addition, we had a very fine cook, the cause of our household being the envy of the entire campus. He cooked the most divine Chinese food, which I always ordered for my birthday party, and curries. Unfortunately, I was not appreciative of the rest of his cuisine, and dallied over my food until the rest of the family had finished and left the table. (You had to finish your food!) When this happened I took my partially full plate and dumped the contents into the nearby pot-bellied stove. The servants certainly knew about this but never let on to my parents. I relate this story to my youngest grandson when he is confronted by the same problem, but where he lives there is no pot-bellied stove. We also had a coolie, whose job was keeping the house clean and tidy. He was the one who always knew where my mother had left her keys. She used to hoard the canned goods, which were very hard to come by, the coffee, tea, and sugar and other condiments and keep them under lock and key so that no servant could touch them without her supervision. However, they all knew where to find her keys, often when she didn't, but nothing was ever missing. Finally there was a woman who used to appear every day to empty the toilets. We had running water, but not flush toilets, and she used to sell the contents to farmers who spread them on their fields. You can understand why we never ate anything uncooked. The use of the terms "boy" and "coolie" is indicative of the colonial atmosphere in which we lived.

The campus of St. John's was not particularly large but it had some of the usual amenities of a college, such as athletic fields, a gym with a swimming pool, and a nine-hole pitch and putt golf course. The course was neatly laid out and well maintained, as the college employed a large staff of gardeners to keep the grounds looking neat. The four grass tennis courts were also well tended. Both the golf course and the tennis courts were reserved for the faculty and their families, and I learned to play golf of sorts and tennis at an early age. The campus was surrounded on three sides by Soochow Creek, an important waterway connecting downtown Shanghai and Suzhou, with a large volume of traffic. Most of this traffic was small boats that were either rowed or poled, though several times a day a steam launch towing four to six of these sampans and belching clouds of black smoke would make its way either up or down stream. A large number of these craft hauled "night soil" or human excrement, loaded in town and eventually to be used as fertilizer on the rice paddies up country. Few of the homes in residential Shanghai had flush toilets, and since the water table was only a few feet, a sewer system was difficult to install. None of the homes or dormitories on the campus had such modern facilities, so St. John's was a good source of nutrients for the rice farmers.

The fourth side of the campus was enclosed by a ten-foot barbed wire fence and two gates. The big gate, which was used for general access, had a large gatehouse and guards who used to operate the gates for incoming and outgoing vehicles. The little gate was at the opposite end of the fence, and I had one of the few keys to the padlock; I used the little gate when I rode my bike to school.

VACATIONS

To escape the worst of the summer humidity, my parents would arrange for the family to get away to a resort either on the coast or in the mountains of Japan. Tsingtao (Qingdao, as it is now known) was a favorite. It had beautiful beaches and mountains nearby. During the age of imperialism, the nineteenth century in particular, this area was the sphere of influence of Imperial Germany and the town to this day reflects the heavy Germanic architecture of that period. After World War I, it became the Japanese "sphere." Throughout it was the mecca for the expatriate community of Shanghai and Beijing and all missionary posts in between. After a few delightful vacations spent in borrowed or rented quarters, my father designed and built a house of our own that was delightfully accommodating, and that could also house not only a family of six but guests and particularly two of the four servants of the household, who came along to service us. When the time came for us to depart for Qingdao we were all loaded on a Japanese coaster for the overnight trip. These were express ships, very fast, and served ports from Shanghai to Dalian (Dairen as it was known then, or Port Arthur when it was part of the czarist "sphere").

I always looked forward to these vacations, but to my great disappointment, after about four years my father decided that summering in one place was boring and sold the house, and from then on we vacationed in a variety of places, including Karuizawa, where my mother had spent holidays when she was growing up in Tokyo, and Nojiri, which was another choice spot on a lake in central Japan and a favorite of expatriates stationed in Japan. It had a lovely lake and a highly competitive sailboat-racing season. The story ends on an ironic note: the money from the sale of the Qingdao house was invested in the American Oriental Bank, managed by a man named Frank Raven. A couple of years later the bank went bankrupt and my father was never able to recover his investment. Mr. Raven was indicted by the American judge in Shanghai and sentenced to prison in Seattle. For him to be sentenced by an American judge in China was possible under the terms of the treaty of extraterritoriality that the Chinese justifiably considered the West's greatest infringement on their sovereignty.

One of the more adventuresome vacations took place in the summer of 1936. I was the only child left at home and was old enough to accompany my parents. We took a Japanese express ship to Fusan (now Pusan), the major port of Chosen (now Korea). These place-names reflect the fact that Korea had been a colony of Japan since early in the twentieth century, and most of the principal towns bore Japanese rather than Korean names. One positive accomplishment by the Japanese was to install a broad network of railways and to run an efficient system of passenger trains. We took advantage of this and traveled extensively. I remember little about Keijo (Seoul) or Heijo (Pyongyang), but have good recollections of spending a week at the oceanside resort of Gensan (Wonsan), which was a favorite vacation spot for expatriates (mostly European and American missionaries) working in the country. Even more memorable was a trek in the Kongosan (otherwise known at the time as the "Diamond Mountains"). I have no idea what this mountain range is presently called, as both it and Wonsan are north of the line separating North and South Korea. The well-maintained trails were dotted with tea houses and inns; some of the ascents were quite steep, but with steps carved out of the rock. I recall elderly women in kimono and geta negotiating them with apparent ease. We spent several days tramping through the mountains. I bought a wooden hiking staff that was branded with a hot iron bearing a distinctive logo at each of the teahouses and inns where we stopped.

We then moved further north to Manchukuo or Manchuria, which had been occupied by the Japanese a few years earlier and since the end of World War II has been reintegrated into China. I remember Mukden (Shenyang) as a rather dour city populated by a large Russian-Czarist community. It was, at that time, one of the most industrialized cities in mainland East Asia. Years later, I heard many tales about the hardships of these White Russians and how they had been abused by the Japanese from my Russian language teacher. I had been sent by the U.S. Army to Oregon State College to learn Russian, which I didn't because the teacher was more interested in telling stories about refugee Russians in English.

From Manchuria we took a train in a southwesterly direction towards Peking (Beijing), but took a brief detour to the resort town of Peitaho (Bei-da-he), which was frequented by the north China expatriate communities: diplomats from Beijing, business people from Tianjin, and missionaries from all over. By now, we had experienced all the major R and R stations in East Asia. Bei-da-he in those days was a Euro/American only resort. Chinese were kept out by a fence that ran across the beach and into the ocean, a practice which was not at all uncommon in China at that time: sort of the last gasp of western imperialism. In a complete turnabout, as was characteristic of the last half of the twentieth century, the resort has become the favorite summer gathering place of the elite of the Chinese People's Republic, where notables gather to socialize and to hold party strategy meetings. Leaders have set up villas and foreigners are not welcome at the resort.

In 1936, Beijing was relatively untouched from the days of the Manchu emperors. The wealthier neighborhoods were dominated by hutongs, which were compounds occupied by large extended families. Some were large enough to accommodate fifty to sixty family members plus numerous retainers. The living quarters formed a U with a large central plaza planted with flowers, dwarf trees, and stylized rock formations. The foreign language school was located in one of these; ironically "foreign language" was actually the Chinese language and the students were non-Chinese; most were missionaries of recent arrival who were to be assigned "up country." I understand that this meaning has been reversed today; foreign means English, Russian, Japanese, etc. Each of us (father, mother, Didi) had his/her own rickshaw. These were much nicer vehicles than those one could hire on the street, sort of like the difference between a limo and a taxi. The seats were softly cushioned and covered with white cases that appeared to have been washed each night. Spokes were nickel plated as were the lanterns on each of the fenders.

We had the run of the city, since this was before the age of Asian tourism, quite a contrast from my next visit forty-seven years later. However, the buildings of the Forbidden City, the Temple of Heaven, and the Summer Palace had not been spruced up for the tourists and many were in a state of disrepair. As an American missionary, my father was interested in inspecting two institutions that had been built with funding from the Boxer rebellion return indemnity. The vanquished Chinese after the Boxer rebellion of 1899 were required to pay the victorious allies a large sum, and the Americans used their portion to fund Yenching University and the Peking Union Medical School, both of which had earned enviable reputations.

Although I have quite vivid recollections of the trip as far as Beijing, I don't remember how we got back to Shanghai. Train travel in China was problematic and the route from Beijing to Nanjing only built in the 1930s. A rail line connected Beijing to Hankow (now part of Wuhan), but the principal connection north from Nanjing was the Grand Canal, famous as the route used to carry tribute from satrapies in Southeast Asia.

There were other trips to various parts of eastern China: to Suchow, Wusih, Yangzhou, and towns in between. I particularly remember Suchow (Suzhou) as the Venice of China. It is not very far from Shanghai, but there is no direct route except by boat up the Grand Canal. My father, however, liked to drive so we took a rather circuitous route via a town which I remembered as Zangzuk (something like that, for the Shanghai dialect was never romanized the way Mandarin was under the Wade-Giles rubric. The town is now called Changshu). Suzhou is the embodiment of the classical intellectual China, much the same way as Beijing is the embodiment of the imperial. To a large extent Suzhou has been spoiled by industrialization. Many of its canals have been filled in and paved over. Classical gardens have been destroyed to make way for factories and high-rise workers' housing.

As the treasurer and general manager of the American Church Mission, my father used to visit the outlying stations, and sometimes took me along. He was the principal

Southeast Asia in the 1930's

RUSSIA

MONGOLIA

Manchukuo

Sea of Japan

JAPAN

Peking

CHINA

Heijo

Wonsan

CHOSEN

Akita

Keijo

Fusan

Karuizawa

Tsingtao

Yellow River

Yellow Sea

Tokyo

Osaka

Kobe

Nanking

Shanghai

Yangtze River

East China Sea

Pacific Ocean

Canton

FORMOSA

North

South China Sea

0   250   500
Miles

PHILIPPINES

Key

Occupied by Japan

administrator for all Episcopalian activity in China and the Philippines. Besides being auditor, he was travel agent, problem solver, and personnel counselor. He took care of the material problems; the emotional and psychological problems were left to the bishop. A missionary's life in China was not always easy, particularly up country, and in many cases new arrivals to the field had little advance notice of what they would experience. A few didn't last very long, and it was my father's job to get them safely back to the United States. He was also the official greeter to new arrivals, many of whom were on their way to these up country assignments. We had a spacious home and some would spend a few days with us before going on. Transportation to and from China was exclusively by boat—I don't recall anyone coming overland from Europe—and Shanghai was the port of entry; there was a lot of coming and going and my parents were in the midst of it. My mother was an energetic and gracious hostess, with abundant servants, including a world-class cook.

China was divided up among western nations into spheres of influence, with the French claiming the south—except for Hong Kong—bordering Indo-China, the English in the Yangtze valley, and Germans in the north, in that part of Shandong near Tsingtao (Quingdao). Missionaries from these nations usually followed their country's imperial designs. Catholics and Americans ignored any boundaries and located where they wished. Episcopalians, being a branch of the Church of England, kept to the Yangtze valley, and my father acted as the liaison between the denominations. My favorite house guests were a pair of jovial Anglican Bishops, Norris and Scott.

EDUCATION

Life at St. John's was about as idyllic as it could get in China.

We had wonderful housing with great expanses of lawn. Our house was about fifty feet from the green of the eighth hole of the nine-hole golf course. We had tennis courts and a gym with a swimming pool. I was lifeguard for two summers during those hours when the pool was reserved for faculty families. There must have been about fifteen American families living on the campus, and neither I nor my older siblings lacked playmates.

My education began at a Chinese kindergarten located on the St John's campus, where we were taught in Chinese and I learned to write characters with a brush, no less. In retrospect, today this would be called a daycare center. The following year I was enrolled in first grade at the Shanghai American School (SAS). SAS was one of the first and largest of the overseas American schools. In subsequent years many of these schools, which are equipped with the standard American pre-college curriculum, have been established in cities abroad to accommodate children of expatriate Americans as well as others who expect to attend colleges in the United States.

While in primary school, my St John's schoolmates and I were driven to school in a taxi, usually with the same driver and the same car, a Model A Ford. The driver used to take great delight in plowing through roadside puddles and splashing pedestrians, particularly young women. If he doused one he would shout out for our benefit: "goodie-no-goodie" and laugh uproariously as he sped on. I have mixed feelings about these antics, and I have no recollection if we encouraged him or not. After grade school, I graduated to a bicycle, to allow me to participate in the many extracurricular activities at SAS. My bicycle route was a varied one: through a crowded Chinese village just outside of St. John's, then across a stinking canal (into which I once fell), around some rice paddy fields, through a high-income residential area, and along some traffic-congested streets patrolled by Sikh traffic cops. I became proficient at dodging rickshaws, wheelbarrows, jaywalkers, other bicyclists, trolley buses, and the occasional truck or car. Bicycles were all licensed and if the police caught you violating traffic rules, they would confiscate your license. Chinese peasants who came to town to sell their produce used to think that if they crossed the street just in front of a speeding car, the car would run over and kill the evil spirit that was perpetually following them. This practice led to an occasional casualty, not of the spirit, but of the peasant.

In the years before World War II, the Shanghai American School was a keen reflection of the life of Shanghai. It was located on a large parcel of land in the French Concession, surrounded by a high fence with guarded entrances. On this campus were built five large buildings in the Federal style, so characteristic of academic institutions in the United States. The principal building used for administration and classrooms was topped by a cupola with a weather vane. Other buildings connected by a colonnade were also of red brick, each housing a girls' and a boys' dormitory. Another building in the same style contained a dining facility, music studios, and maintenance offices. Several years before the outbreak of hostilities, a building housing a fine auditorium and additional classrooms was completed. This must have been in 1940, as I recall a senior class play being featured at the opening. These structures were arranged around a quadrangle, where much of the daytime social activity took place during pleasant weather. The main center of activity was the gym, which was well equipped with a basketball court and exercise areas. It also contained locker rooms and showers, separate, of course, for boys and girls, and offices for coaches. There were portable grandstands for basketball fans. Perhaps the most identifying feature was the water tower, which stood taller than the surrounding buildings. It too was built of brick and was topped with a sloping slate roof. There were a number of auxiliary buildings and quarters for the Chinese staff. Two such buildings that I remember well were the kindergarten–first grade building, which was located away from the rest of the buildings with its own playground. The other structure was the bicycle house, where those of us who biked to school could leave our cycles under guard. As we wheeled our bikes into the building, little more than a shed, the guard would give us a numbered brass tag, which we endeavored not to lose during the day.

Basketball, track, and swimming drew crowds of spectators. I participated in almost all of the sports. The school was equipped with really first class playing fields, of which there were three, a quarter-mile track, sand pits for high jump and pole vault, and good quality tennis courts. The sports that were offered were basketball, six-man football, soccer (I was captain my senior year), track (I ran the 440-yard low hurdles and put the shot), softball, and swimming. I longed to make the varsity basketball team because that attracted the most coeds and the cheerleaders were close by. Furthermore basketball had an international dimension, which was not a feature of other sports. There was an annual game with the Canadian Academy from Kobe, which was a very glamorous affair. Athletics were an important part of campus life, and interscholastic competition in soccer drew spectators from the community at large. Until my senior year I was relegated to the junior varsity, whose games attracted no spectators; for reasons I explain later, I was jerked from the team in mid-season.

Non-sport extracurricular activities attracted lots of participants. I was sports editor for the *SAS Nooz*, which became the *Shanghai American*, a weekly student newspaper. The *Columbian* was the slick annual all-student publication. Dramatics were an important activity. I once played a very minor role in *The Importance of Being Ernest*. The school had a marching band, an orchestra, and a choral group. If I had a copy of the 1941 *Columbian*, I could probably cite several other clubs I belonged to, but since I never graduated in Shanghai, at the time the publication came out, I never received one.

The culture and the curriculum were the typically American college preparatory type, appropriate for the time and copied from those of the American prep school. Until I reached the eleventh grade, there was no course in the schedule available that dealt with China. There was no instruction in the Chinese language. I learned that instruction in Chinese culture was offered to some students on an ad hoc basis, but this was not known to the student body at large. As juniors, some fellow students and I agitated for a course in Chinese history to be included as a formal offering. I agreed to take the case to the principal, which was not difficult, as by that time the principal had married my sister. Recently I have learned that the situation has changed dramatically and that courses dealing with China are a requirement and that two years of Chinese language are also required to graduate.

The student body was predominantly American. Not until I reached high school did I have any Chinese classmates, and potential students from other expatriate communities had their own schools. A few non-American expats did enroll (I had Danish friends, and there were Russians and Jewish refugees from Nazi Germany) but these were intent in going to the States for college. Children of mixed—Chinese and foreign—unions were looked down upon and did not attend the pure expat schools. Rather they wound up at Saint Xavier, a Jesuit school.

Social life was "bifurcated." Children of staunch missionaries, mostly boarders, led a restricted social life, primarily without dancing. Seldom were there parties and other social events scheduled on campus. Class parties and similar high school events were usually held off campus at the American Women's Club. However, by the time I was a senior, this situation was beginning to ease up, and these restrictions no longer are in effect. The "day hops" on the other hand led a social life similar to that in the United States. Most of the day hops were children of business, diplomatic, or academic families, even though the latter were missionary institutions such as St. John's and the University of Shanghai. Dating was frequent and the girlfriend-boyfriend system was quite obvious.

Much as I envied my male acquaintances who dated regularly, I was out of the loop, as I lived too far away from the school or too distant from the American club and the part of Shanghai where most of the expatriates lived. I was invited to and eagerly attended dance parties given by parents of classmates, but always alone. I had no access to a car, and trying to team up with someone who had a date and who did have access was next to impossible considering where I lived. Having a date ride on the back of my bicycle was out of the question. I did have one friendly female classmate named Peggy with whom I shared political activity. In our junior year we ran as a ticket for class president and vice president and were elected, and reelected the following year. Several weeks into our senior year, the president of the student body was evacuated because of the threat of the outbreak of war, and I ran successfully for the vacancy. When I was evacuated several months later, she was elected to replace me.

I did enjoy one social occasion with Peggy on New Year's Eve 1940–41. As a guest of her parents, I joined Peggy and her socially prominent parents nightclub crawling to places I had never seen the inside of. As midnight approached we were in the dance club of the Astor House, the most exclusive night club in Shanghai, well hatted and equipped with appropriate noisemakers. I must add that neither Peggy nor I was offered any alcoholic drinks. As dawn broke, I was dropped off at the front gate of the St. John's campus and ran home in time for breakfast and to grab my golf clubs and appear at the first hole for the New Year's golf tournament. I won a trophy for my play in that tournament. Peggy and I did date a few times later when we were freshmen in college: she at Bennington and I at Williams less than twenty miles away. However I was soon drafted and did not get back to college for another four and a half years, and of course she had long gone. I did encounter Peggy at a Shanghai American School reunion in New York; we were each happily married with several children.

As described later, I was no longer in Shanghai at the time of graduation. Unfortunately I had no choice in the matter and I departed very reluctantly because I had started my senior year as class president, but subsequently was elected chair of the Senate when my predecessor was evacuated, was captain of the soccer team, and so considered myself as a feature on campus.

ENCOUNTERS WITH THE WORLD

In contrast to life in Shanghai were the furloughs we took every five years. As a missionary serving in a "heathen" country, my father was given a furlough, which usually lasted from six to eight months, once every five years. His objective, besides reporting to the U.S. headquarters of the Episcopal establishment in New York, was to visit relatives in the United States. In order to spend the most time with his relatives, particularly his aged mother, we took a passenger ship as directly as possible across the Pacific. I recall being on three of these furloughs. I was too young to remember anything about the first one.

The second was a reversal of this pattern. This furlough took us by ship from Shanghai to Genoa, stopping at a variety of exotic ports along the way: Hong Kong, Manila, Belawan in Sumatra, Colombo, Djibouti, Port Said. The German ship, carrying both passengers and cargo, was in no hurry and we were able to see some of the local sights along the way. Almost all of these I have visited once or more in recent years, noticing the changes over time. The boat trip finally ended in Genoa and after a brief stay in Rome, we headed north to Switzerland.

Once in Europe we traveled extensively by train, focusing particularly on Saxony and Dresden, which had been the home of my maternal grandmother. The year was 1932, and I can remember distinctly while hiking in the hills on the Saxon-Czech border coming across bands of Hitler youth singing the Horst Wessel song. Another memory was the night we spent in a hotel by the railroad station in Nuremberg when I stayed awake most of the night excitedly watching the shunting engines at work, a new experience for a Shanghai child. Part of that furlough was spent in London; while my parents and older siblings went sightseeing, I was confined to the British Museum, where I learned a great deal about Egyptian mummies and the Elgin Marbles. I also remember getting violently seasick on the trip across the Atlantic, the only time I have ever succumbed aboard ship, yacht, or rowboat, even though the ship was the newest and the fastest transatlantic liner of the day.

The upshot of this round-the-world trip was that we spent little time with American relatives: I remember staying with Uncle Scott on his farm outside of Cape May, New Jersey. He had chickens and orchards and divine asparagus beds. Two activities that involved us kids were making root beer and selling eggs, apples, and peaches from a stand on the highway. This was an important highway running from Cape

May to the New York City area. On many a night we were wakened by the explosion of bottled root beer that we had not capped properly. Living with Scott then was my paternal grandmother, a stern and proper Victorian type for whom I developed little affection (I can't even to this day remember her maiden name) and who thought my father had married below his station and that his children were not being properly brought up in a faraway land inhabited by dark-skinned folk; a contrast to my German grandmother, who was very warm and caring, and was really loved by her Japanese friends, although I rebuffed her efforts to teach me German. In New York my father bought a new Chevrolet, which we drove across to San Francisco. The car was equipped with right-hand drive, as one drove on the left in China. The car attracted considerable curiosity along the way, and when questioned about the steering wheel on the wrong side, he responded that it allowed him to put his arm around his girlfriend and still drive with his right hand. I never fell for this, but that seemed to satisfy the curious.

The last furlough, in 1937, was not eventful, except that I missed part of the school year and I had to repeat the ninth grade when I got back to Shanghai. I was sent to summer camp in the Poconos, which was a new experience for me and one that I was unable to acclimate to. The major counselors were Army types from Virginia Military Institute and they tried to run the place like a boot camp. Most campers took this in stride, because they were repeaters, but it was very strange to me. The waterfront counselor finally indulged me by making me his assistant, which consisted of my rowing the boat while he kept in shape by swimming across the lake and back.

In the fall we moved into the upper floor of an old house on Spruce Street in West Philadelphia. The bathroom was located off a landing between the two floors. The house was close to the campus of the University of Pennsylvania and located just across Spruce Street from the dental school. In those days a noisy street car that ran along Spruce Street tended to keep me awake at night, but also meant a short trip to West Philadelphia High School, where I was enrolled in the ninth grade. The school administration had trouble with my name, so I was known as "Walter Millidge." The classes were so large and the school so crowded that by the time I learned my way around, we needed to leave for home. I do remember that students could only go one way in the hall because the traffic between classes was so heavy. I have a distinct recollection of attending my first intercollegiate football game between Cornell and Penn. I was taken to the game as a guest of the son of the then-mayor of that part of Shanghai apart from the Settlement and the Concession, who had been a student in my mother's German class at St. John's.

My parents did a fair amount of traveling, to visit other relatives on both sides of the family, and I was not to be left alone in the rented rooms. On these occasions, I was sent to stay with my rich uncle William and his family who lived in Merion, one of the ritziest suburbs on the Philadelphia Main Line. His stepson (William and Anna, his wife, each had a child from previous marriage) was my age and attended a very prestigious prep school in the neighborhood. Obviously our respective school experiences were very different and we had little in common. I later encountered him as a fellow freshman at Williams College, but for all his prep-school experience (and the bulk of the undergraduate boys at Williams came from exclusive prep schools), he didn't last the year. However, he did have an illustrious career as a B-17 pilot during World War II, with many missions over western Europe. His stepsister, my cousin, was a lovely girl for whom I had a brief crush. I do remember that Uncle William, who managed a licorice-importing company located across the river in New Jersey that was obviously was quite successful (licorice was a very important ingredient for holding together the tobacco in cigarettes), owned a Cadillac and a LaSalle, long before German imports became the luxury vehicles. I also remember that when it came time for either of these cars to be serviced, a guy would come by on a three-wheeled motorcycle, hitch it to the rear bumper and take off, returning later in the afternoon again with the car and the cycle in tow. This kind of service was not provided for Chevrolets, or for the Studebaker that my father had bought to drive across the continent and take to China.

By the time we were scheduled to return to Shanghai in early 1938, the Sino-Japanese war had started and there was some hesitation about going back. However, the Japanese seemed unwilling to provoke the international community by occupying the International Settlement or the French Concession and my father thought it safe to return. I was the only child on this trip as my siblings were either through college, in college, or about to enter. The return trip again featured a cross-country drive in my father's newly acquired Studebaker, also equipped with right-hand drive. As it was winter, we took the southern route; I do remember going through El Paso to San Diego. We were briefly delayed as we encountered snow in the Siskiyou mountains of southern Oregon. My father had never experienced snow on the road before, and couldn't handle the snow-covered highway. A tow truck finally hauled us out of the snowbank with little damage to the car.

From Vancouver we took the *S.S. Empress* of Japan for the leisurely trip across the Pacific with stops in Honolulu, Yokohama, and Kobe, and at each port visited with family friends. I have a vivid impression of developing a crush on a female fellow passenger, Miriam LaFollette, daughter of the then Senator Robert LaFollette. I recall her as a very attractive young woman, several years older than I, and although she was very friendly, there were several older men who paid her close attention who could stay up later, and I was very awkward on the dance floor. At that age, crushes came easily to me.

In retrospect, these furloughs were a worthwhile learning experience, but in the long run, I got to know less about America than about the rest of the world. The American experiences were too brief and infrequent, so that little rubbed off on me. This was particularly evident when I came to the States to briefly complete my high school education and to prepare for entry to college. I was a foreigner.

CHAPTER TWO

College and War

T HE PRELIMINARY SKIRMISHES BETWEEN THE CHI-
nese and Japanese that had been occurring off and on
since 1927 eventually intensified by 1937 to be called the
Sino-Japanese war. The effort became called, for propaganda
purposes, "The Greater East Asia Co-Prosperity Sphere."
Although the International Settlement and the French Concession had been spared any direct attack by the Japanese,
the Japanese military had virtually commandeered that part
of the Settlement called Hongkew where most Chinese lived.
The other foreign powers were allowed to maintain their
armed forces in and around Shanghai. In the case of the St.
John's campus, well outside the boundaries of the Settlement,
there was a battalion of British troops stationed right across
the street. We were well aware of their presence, as we could
hear their bugle calls and band practice quite clearly, and, of
course we were very grateful for their presence. His Majesty's
soldiers would drill in the neighboring Jessfield Park along
with the marching band. The garrison was rotated regularly,
and on various occasions the "Tommies," as they were called,

39

came from Scottish regiments and drilled in their kilts, playing bagpipes. All this was going on with the Japanese and Chinese exchanging fire not half a mile away.

As Japan was becoming increasingly friendly with the Axis powers fighting in Europe, the U.S. State Department became deeply concerned that the Japanese would launch some kind of hostilities against the United States and strongly suggested that all nonessential Americans seek sanctuary somewhere outside of East Asia: the United States, Australia, and some Latin American country were suggested. A sequence of large transpacific ocean liners from the American President Lines and the Matson Lines were rerouted to ports in China and the Philippines.

My father, who by this time had become the business manager of all Episcopal and Anglican missionary activities in China and the Philippines, felt obligated to set an example by scheduling his wife and dependent son to take one of these ships. My mother left Shanghai in December of 1940 for the United States and I expected to stay on in Shanghai until I graduated with my class in June 1941. For reasons he never convincingly explained to me, perhaps under pressure from his missionary constituency, in March I found myself aboard the *President Hoover* bound for San Francisco. I have vivid memories of that crossing as I commiserated with some schoolmates over having to leave SAS before the glamorous events at the end of the school year: proms and other parties and commencement. Also aboard was the semi-professional Twentieth Century Fox basketball team, which had just played a series of exhibition games in Manila. They allowed me to shoot baskets with them.

Remaining in Shanghai was my father, who for health reasons was himself evacuated to the states in June, and my older brother, Henry, who had no connection to St. John's or the mission and who was on his own, having obtained a degree in electrical engineering from Stevens Institute of Technology. Henry was working at the Shanghai Power Company and eventually was interned by the Japanese military for four and a half years.

I joined my mother, who was living in a rather shabby apartment in Morningside Heights in New York City, near Columbia University, and found myself enrolled at Horace Mann School for Boys. The only reason I could discern for selecting this school was its connection to Columbia, and my sister Betty and her husband Ray, the former principal of SAS, were in the graduate program at Teachers College, Columbia University. Horace Mann was located in Riverdale, at the northern extremity of New York City, a rather lengthy ride on the subway to Van Cortlandt Park. Two very friendly classmates who lived in the Morningside neighborhood showed me the ropes of subway riding, and the three of us often rode together. At Horace Mann I joined the track team, participating in the shot put and the 440 yards low hurdles.

I did graduate despite the interruption and culture shock, and at the commencement exercises the presentation of diplomas was interrupted with the announcement by the headmaster that he was having another dignitary present the diploma of the Shanghai American School to a refugee. This dignitary was my brother-in-law. Of course graduation was not complete without the senior prom and I was persuaded by some fellow seniors to attend with a blind date. I had never previously dated and a blind date was overwhelming. I was to pick her up at what I thought was a very fancy hotel on Central Park South. I checked in at the hotel and was informed that my date lived on the seventh floor. Not knowing the proper procedure, I went to her apartment rather than waiting in the lobby. There I was met by a rather sour faced parent who instructed me in proper deportment and sent me packing back to the lobby. I was so embarrassed by the episode that I have no recollection how the rest of the evening transpired.

Over the summer I learned a little more about life in the States by working as a receiving clerk in a department store in Poughkeepsie, New York. What I remember about that job was operating a machine that pinned price tags on women's underwear. I was paid the munificent sum of $9 a week. I was living with my aunt Abigail and uncle George Landis and their four daughters so that room and board cost me nothing. They had just acquired a cottage and two small sailboats on Lake Candlewood in western Connecticut. I knew a little about handling a small boat, so I managed to take it out on the lake at every opportunity. On one occasion while I was sailing singlehandedly I rammed a Star boat, which is lightly built for racing. In any event, I had to pay for the repairs, and there went all the nine-dollar sums I had saved over the summer.

That fall I started my freshman year at Williams College, located in a rather remote northwestern corner of Massachusetts. A small elite men's college was strange and confusing to me. The most noticeable of the students were from prominent prep schools and carried these attitudes and behavior patterns with them into college. Williams was not large enough to have the diversity of a major university and I failed to adapt to the dominant culture. There was no Asian course where I might have been able to show my advantage. After Pearl Harbor many classmates decided to leave college to enlist, and they seemed to have the choice of the Navy or Marines. Those of us who decided to stay in college were enrolled into the "enlisted reserve," which, we were told, would allow us to finish our accelerated college program. That turned out to be a typical Army SNAFU and we were called up within six months. In retrospect, I doubt I was mature enough to handle college life, and despite being brought up in a foreign country, was not cosmopolitan enough to adapt easily to a different lifestyle. By the same measure, was I equipped to handle life in the Army?

My Army career lasted almost four and a half years, none of it even coming close to combat. I started out in the ski troops, then based at Camp Hale in Colorado, which was located in a basin where a lake had been filled in to create the army camp. After my first turn at basic training (I was to have two more), I was told that I was unfit for general duty because of my poor eyesight. I was given the position of "armorer and artificer" in an infantry company, but I never learned what responsibilities I had. My only real accomplishment was to build a stand next to the mess hall for trash containers. I did spend much time in the supply room cleaning and oiling machine guns and mortars, which I thought was a better job than cook's helper, and I did get promoted to corporal. Some officer in the ranks of the decision makers, or perhaps the battalion chaplain, decided that I should be in intelligence because of my China background. I was assigned to regimental S2, which did get me out of the supply room and for reasons I could never fathom, got me the job of assistant to the rock climbing instructor. My function was superfluous, but I taught the trainees how to tie knots, and what pitons and carabiners were used for in climbing up the face of a cliff.

There was a payoff, for within the month I was transferred to language school under the Army Specialized Training Program. I thought I was to be sent to Yale, which had a Chinese program, but instead I headed west to Corvallis, Oregon, and was assigned to study Russian. When I protested that I knew no Russian, but was fluent in Shanghai street talk, I was told not to worry, I would be studying Siberian Russian. I learned little Russian, but had a delightful time at Oregon State College, where all the males, having joined ROTC, were serving their country, and the females were yearning for company. The Russian teacher was Nina Fedorova, who not long before had won the Atlantic Monthly Prize for her novel *The Family* about life among the White Russian émigrés living in Manchuria under the oppressive domination of the Japanese. She had also spent some time in Shanghai, so we spent most of the time exchanging experiences in English. While at Oregon State, which in those days was the typical "cow college," I dated a coed from Portland. As our friendship grew, she asked me to accompany her to Portland to meet her family and particularly her aunt, who had spent some time in China. We took the bus to Portland and I was duly presented to her family. The aunt dropped by the next day and to my great surprise, she turned out to have been my Latin teacher from SAS. Since I had not done well in her course, our meeting was somewhat muted and over the next few weeks I noticed a definite cooling-off in my relationship with the coed. I guess I was considered not a good catch. But then, there were lots of other girls on campus looking for male companionship.

This idyllic life was not to last; after five months I found myself back in an infantry regiment and after my second basic training was assigned to the regimental cavalry reconnaissance troop of the 70th infantry division stationed at Camp Adair near Corvallis: no horses, but armored cars, halftracks, and personnel carriers. We were told that our stay on the college campus was terminated because every available body was required to participate in the oncoming invasion of continental Europe. The troop's current assignment was to patrol the coast of Oregon and to report on any suspicious enemy naval activity in coastal waters. Much later I learned that the Oregon shore had been approached by Japanese mini submarines, one of which had launched balloon-borne incendiaries intended to start forest fires. One of these bombs actually killed a woman picnicking with her family in one of the state parks. She was the only war fatality in the forty-eight contiguous states.

However this version of events was questioned years later when research on Japanese efforts to launch gas-filled balloons to cross the Pacific on prevailing west-to-east winds carrying incendiary and explosive-loaded devices revealed that they were occasionally successful and that Japanese warships had never launched such balloons. But this coastal patrolling turned out to be a cushy assignment as we drove up and down U.S. Route 101 in Jeeps and half-tracks and bivouacked on the beach each night after inflating rubber boats and fishing in the surf.

Meanwhile, I had applied for further language study, hoping all along that this time the Army would get it right by sending me to Yale to study Chinese. However, that was not to be and I wound up at the University of Michigan to study Japanese at the Army Japanese Language Program, part of the Military Intelligence branch of the army. This was the army's counter to the Navy program at Boulder, Colorado, which was older and better organized. The Navy participants received commissions as ensigns before they entered, while we were commissioned as second lieutenants only after we finished. Spoken Chinese and Japanese have little in common, and although the Japanese use Chinese characters, their pronunciation is usually quite different. I never thought my Chinese background was any help in learning Japanese, and there were a number of us born-in-China types in the same boat.

The instruction was quite intensive, no fooling around with personal histories. Some of our instructors had very little English capability, so the conduct of the classes was in Japanese exclusively. The class, labeled "May 45," which was the date we were to finish the program, consisted of about thirty enlisted men, divided up into sections of five or six and ranked depending on how well we were learning the language. Classes were held five days a week with a quiz (shiken in Japanese) every Saturday morning. If you did well on the quiz, you were promoted to the next level; if you did poorly, your place was taken by the best of a lower level. It was a very stressful situation and there were a couple of suicides before we completed the course eighteen months later.

By this time any affection between me and the Oregon girl had come to an end, but dates on the U of M campus were not difficult to find, again because civilian males were a rarity. The first date I had with a sorority girl was somewhat unique, when the boat in which I took her sailing capsized. The mishap, although it had us wet and shivering, warmed our relationship, which continued for the six months at the university and about three months after the program ended. I was assigned elsewhere when I got a letter saying that my letters contained nothing but complaints about Army life and that she had met a Navy ensign and had plans to marry him. I assumed that rank played a role in this distancing and perhaps a Naval officer had less to complain about.

The course at Ann Arbor lasted an academic year, after which the group of students were sent to Ft. McClellan in Alabama for basic training—the third time for me after the first in Camp Hale, Colorado, and the second at Camp Adair in Oregon. This experience was somewhat of a sham, as we were considered as "smart ass" intellectuals, difficult to control and unwilling to be trained, which was an accurate assessment. The next stop was Fort Snelling in Minnesota, where we were to learn advanced Japanese focusing on order of battle, whatever that was, so that we could interrogate Japanese prisoners of war. That winter was very cold, particularly when we drilled on the parade ground high above the Mississippi River, exposed to gusty north winds. I got to be company guide, who marched at the head of the company as a wind break for the rest. Fort Snelling was at the end of the trolley line and it was easy to get to downtown Minneapolis and to warm up in the bars on Hennepin Avenue. Since we were no longer on a college campus, dates were more difficult to find: one at the University of Minnesota, another at Carlton College in Northfield, and a third at Eau Claire Teachers College in Wisconsin. By the time we completed this segment of our training, the war was over and the graduates of the language program were given the option of taking a discharge or receiving a commission and going to Japan with the occupation.

OCCUPIED IN JAPAN

By this time my command of the language was pretty extensive and I chose the latter, spending almost two years in Japan. Only a few of us graduates of the Army Japanese Language School went to Japan and as starters were assigned to ATIS (Allied Translation and Interpretation Service) in Tokyo, a very dull job where we checked the English translations of newspaper articles done by Japanese of limited English ability. Quickly tiring of this, I was able to transfer, by means I have forgotten, perhaps because I spoke Japanese, to the Counter Intelligence Corps, whose major job at that time was to keep track of the members of the top officers of the Imperial Military Command who were not already in detention awaiting trial for war crimes.

One of the chief sources of information about these senior officers came from the JCP (Japanese Communist Party), which was only too eager to have its members keep these military commanders under surveillance. Keeping in touch with the leaders of the JCP, particularly Nosaka Sanzo, was a great pleasure. I met him in the party headquarters in Shinjuku about once a week to chat and get reports on the movements of the military elite. Occasionally we would create an excuse to raid one of these generals' villas, finding no incriminating evidence but boxes full of pornographic books, pictures, and ceramic figurines. Contact with the JCP was not to last, for the MacArthur command and particularly its G2 intelligence section, commanded by Gen. Charles Willoughby, became increasingly convinced that the communists, not the militarists, were the principal enemy. General Willoughby, who claimed to come from a prominent Prussian Junker family, was called "my lovable fascist" by General MacArthur. The last time I emerged from the JCP headquarters, I was arrested by MPs and detained overnight until my commanding officer was able to bail me out. I assume that the MPs thought me to be a communist sympathizer, and since as a counter intelligence agent I wore no military insignia, which was the normal garb for civilians working for the military, the MPs were unsure of my status.

One of the reasons for this change of mind by SCAP (Supreme Commander Allied Powers) was the threat of strike by the railway workers union. One of the occupation objectives was to replicate American institutions in Japan, including legislatures, political parties, large-scale businesses, and labor unions among others. Organizers from the CIO were sent to Japan to help in setting up unions, and the most successful was the railway workers union. At one point in the summer of 1946, the union decided to go on strike. Railways were important to the U.S. army and a strike would be inconvenient as road transportation was practically non-existent in those days. MacArthur summoned the union leaders to his headquarters in the Dai-Ichi Building, shut them up in a conference room, stationed MPs at the doors, and announced that none would leave until a decision not to strike was made. Union leaders gave in after about twelve hours and railroads continued to run. MacArthur was convinced that communists were behind the strike and counter intelligence was to switch from Japanese military to Japanese communists. There was some justification for this because Japanese soldiers who had been taken by the Soviet army in Manchuria and North Korea were now being repatriated, and some of these were believed to have become Soviet agents.

I did have a chance to interrogate several of these repatriated Japanese veterans and found them to be ardent anti-communists, because the Russian military had treated them so harshly that any attempted indoctrination was soundly rejected. But by 1947 the Cold War had begun and an anti-communist tilt pervaded SCAP. CIC was now asked to investigate civilian members of the SCAP headquarters and our job was to keep Americans under surveillance. Most of these foreign experts were housed in two hotels: the famed Imperial Hotel designed by Frank Lloyd Wright for senior civilians and the Dai-Ichi Hotel (not to be confused with the Dai-Ichi building, which housed SCAP) for the juniors. Fortunately by late 1946 I was reassigned to G2 of SCAP and was relieved of having to negotiate crawlspaces and heating ducts to tap the rooms of these hotels.

My recollection of the MacArthur regime was not particularly positive. He tried to promote an image of an imperial self, perhaps as an alternative to the Emperor. There were many in SCAP itself who were convinced that the Emperor was so involved in the policy of military aggression that he should have been tried as a war criminal. MacArthur made sure that this did not happen and in retrospect, the removal of the Emperor would not have changed the course of Japan's postwar recovery.

Life in Japan as a member of the occupying army was somewhat unique. Along with a number of my Japanese-speaking colleagues, I was billeted in what was the former headquarters of the Kempeitai, the Japanese secret service. I had a room in one of the typically Japanese residences attached to the austere office building. The room had paper thin walls and privacy was nonexistent, but the officers club nearby was extensive and well equipped. Although I was offered a Japanese girlfriend, I declined and what's more no Japanese were allowed to frequent the club. An American female civilian employee in G2 and I dated frequently and used the club's facilities regularly. She was a BIJ (born in Japan) who had graduated from the Navy language school, but had taken a discharge to come to Japan. Her family had been acquaintances of my mother's family. We took several trips around Japan together, particularly to Karuizawa, where our respective families had vacationed. Most of these trips were to destinations that were Army sanctioned: to Kyoto, Nara, Nikko, Akita, and the like, or to other military installations such as a fellow CIC officer's establishment in Shizuoka. Staying in a typical Japanese inn was forbidden, and the one occasion when we broke this rule in a small rustic village we were sought out by military police but the landlady hid us and my Jeep, which had my unit's designation painted on the rear bumper.

CHAPTER THREE

What Kind
of Career

AFTER EIGHTEEN MONTHS IN JAPAN AND SCAP'S
increasing preoccupation with what it believed to be
the undermining of the occupation by procommunist civilian
personnel assigned to the command, I began to seek discharge
and to get back to completing my college education. I doubt
that by the summer of 1947 I was of much use to the occupation, and I had little difficulty securing my release. I was able
to get passage on a military DC7 (I think that was what they
were called) and flew with numerous stops (Guam, Kwajalein,
Johnson Island, Honolulu, and Fairfield-Suisun, California)
across the Pacific. I was given a discharge promotion to First
Lieutenant and hurried back to the Berkshire Hills in western
Massachusetts, first to my parents, who were living in Sheffield, and thence back to Williams.

Williams was extremely generous to give me a whole
year's worth of credit for the language courses I had taken

in the Army; thus I returned as a senior. Hardly any of my former classmates were still on campus, and my preoccupation was to complete the requirements for a degree in political science. Since I was eligible for the GI Bill of Rights, my tuition was covered and since fraternities were still tolerated (they were abolished some fifteen years later, around the time that the college went coed) I was able to wait tables for board. Without having to find other employment, I was able to concentrate on studies.

Two courses stand out from that year: modern art and modern architecture, each taught by eminent scholars in the field: Whitney Stoddard and Lane Faison. I still remember the names and works of artists such as Monet, Renoir, Van Gogh, and Matisse, and architects such as Gropius and Le Corbusier, and can still easily identify their works in galleries and in European and American locations.

I certainly did not graduate with distinction, and my relations with Williams have been very distant. I was cut from the college mailing list after my fifty-fifth reunion, which like all other college reunions I did not attend. I am unsure if I can still claim to be an alumnus of the college. Incidentally, even though I never had any intention of returning to the military, I was talked into signing up for the U.S. Army reserves as an officer in Military Intelligence for seven years. In retrospect, I was lucky not to have been called up during the Korean War, particularly because I was on record as being a fluent speaker of Japanese; by that time I was employed by another intelligence institution of the U.S. government.

The following summer I experienced another unique American experience, that of a camp counselor. The camp was located on one of the many lakes in central Maine, and water sports and boating were features. My principal function was to make sure the boys, ranging from nine to fifteen, behaved themselves and stayed healthy. Otherwise I spent my time painting the mess hall and taking the trash to the community dump. To do the latter, I was provided with a twenty-year-old Plymouth roadster with a flatbed in place of a rumble seat. It worked fine since the dump was less than one and a half miles from the camp driveway—until late in the summer when the vehicle dropped its driveshaft on the way down to the lake. The driveshaft became detached, struck a rock, and lifted the rear wheels about three feet off the ground. This event and another that happened when I was driving the Ford "beach wagon" (as wood-clad station wagons were called in New England) towing a trailer with four fabric-clad canoes aboard, one of which slid to a point just over one of the wheels and received a large gash in its bottom, did not endear me to the camp management. I was relieved of any maintenance functions and assigned as assistant to the waterfront counselor. Needless to say I was not asked to return the following summer. With only hazy plans about the future, I decided to enroll as a graduate student in the Institute of Asian Studies at Columbia University. I had some world class professors, Sir George Samson and Hugh Borton among others, but was not particularly motivated toward more schooling and left after one academic year, having been offered a job in the Central Intelligence Agency. One course I particularly remembered from the year at Columbia was colloquial Chinese. This was a course in Mandarin, in which I had had no previous training, as my knowledge of the language was limited to spoken colloquial Shanghai street talk, at which I was quite fluent. The instructor was a delightful woman, Lily Shang, who was the wife of a military attaché of the Nationalist Chinese government assigned to the UN. In my recitations I often became confused and frequently ended a sentence in the Shanghai dialect or in Japanese. Ms. Shang understood my problem because she knew all three languages I was using, but she was vastly amused at what she heard and had to cover her face with her copy book to hide her laughter from the rest of the class. I realized that this was her effort to prevent me from losing face.

In the summer of 1949 I left New York for Washington, where I joined the "brightest and the best," recruited mainly from Ivy League universities. Why the agency selected me remains a mystery, possibly because of my "Sino Japanese background." In Washington, I was assigned to the China desk but spent most of the time going to various training schools, learning how to write with invisible ink, use mini cameras, make micro dots, and participate in a variety of intelligence scenarios. Fortunately, my assignment was to the Office of Special Operations, whose mission was collecting intelligence and not undermining governments or participating in coups d'état, otherwise known as "clandestine ops." My impression of the activities of the CIA during my very brief career was that its activities were crude and not very effective. A variety of well-informed authors, journalists, and agency veterans have resoundingly criticized the agency, and my brief involvement confirms their views.

Completing training, I was sent over to the State Department to acquire diplomatic cover: Third Secretary and Vice Consul. Consular duties were to be my future, and I learned a lot about sailors who jumped ship or who got into fights in Singapore or Mombasa. I was scheduled to join the Consulate General in Shanghai, but was diverted to New Delhi when all the U.S. missions were closed in China over some dispute with the new People's Republic of China over the Marine Barracks in Beijing. The State Department considered the Marine barracks as diplomatic property and hence immune from seizure by the host government. The Chinese considered the property as a place for housing military and hence not immune. As a result, diplomatic relations were severed and were not restored until after Nixon's visit in 1976.

I found consular duties, at least as they functioned in the State Department, quite boring, but since I had no status within State, I could not roam the halls looking for an alternative assignment. Eventually I was ordered to prepare to go to New Delhi, India; by 1950, I was aboard a Pan American Lockheed Constellation. In those days these flights took more than twenty-four hours and made many stops. The flight was made more pleasant for me because the stewardess, as cabin attendants were then known, was the sister of a SAS classmate of mine and had grown up in Shanghai. From Istanbul on, the seat next to mine was empty so during the long nighttime flight to Tehran we reminisced about life at SAS and Shanghai. She visited New Delhi several times during the next few months but became attracted to the Assistant Air Force Attaché with whom I shared an apartment and eventually married him. The shared apartment replacement was the head of the Embassy communications office.

New Delhi needed a Chinese language officer, I was told, for reasons that escaped me. I did replace an officer who spoke better Chinese than I, because he grew up "up country" where there were few non-Chinese speakers. He informed me that the only Chinese he spoke was to a Chinese Professor at the University of Delhi, and they spent an evening every two weeks conversing in Chinese. Actually I was not assigned to the consular section of the embassy, for the man in charge was named Walker and it was thought that two of the same name would be confusing. I was identified as a political officer and as the most junior officer became responsible for the Embassy's security, which in those days was not much of a job because security was pretty lax.

The Embassy was housed in the palace of the Maharaja of Bahawalpur, a sprawling building on a big lot surrounded by a wall three feet high. Bahawalpur was now in West Pakistan, and since Maharaja was an Indian title, he had lost most of his possessions and this palace was available. Furthermore, princely states were considered to be a creation of the British, and the Government of India was in the process of expropriating them and incorporating the lands into the regular national political configuration. The building was designed with large windows and many French doors to take advantage of any air motion during the hot seasons, which last most of the year in north India. Security in those days was a matter of little concern. All kinds of wires ran every which way and none of the maintenance staff knew what they were for. Each office had an outside door to a colonnade that ran the length of the building, and these doors were not locked. There was a Sikh guard with a double-barreled shotgun that was never loaded; he had a few shells in his pocket that were good for shooting ducks. My job was to see that all three-combination file cabinets were locked up for the night and the display fan turned to the closed position. As I recall, no one was ever disciplined for security violations even though I reported them regularly.

My biggest challenge came with the arrival of the Marine detachment. Marines were supposed to be under the command of the Naval attaché, but he considered himself to be too high ranking to succor these Marines, and since the Marines and I were to secure the Embassy and I was the security officer, I was given the job. The embassy had built a Quonset hut on the spacious grounds as housing for the detachment, one of the most inappropriate building styles considering the climate of New Delhi. I was told to satisfy their complaints and to see that they "made the necessary culture adaptations" for life in India, no simple task under the circumstances. This was a job for which I was not suited and for which my "diplomatic" training had not prepared me. I do remember spending much time trying to mollify irate Marines and to get someone to address their problems. Help was soon to come in the form of air conditioners. Only the Ambassador's office had a real air conditioner; the rest of us had "desert coolers," which consisted of large boxes containing reeds and a fan. Water dripped on the reeds and the fan blew moist air into the room. These were big noisy contraptions, useful only in the hot dry season. During the hot monsoon season they were worse than useless.

My office was located in the seraglio, facing a small stone courtyard surrounded by a high wall for the privacy of the women in the Maharaja's domain. The space was even more airless than other offices, and the wall kept any breezes blowing from the garden from reaching my office. When I first occupied the room, there was a bamboo screen over the door and a rope tied to a little boy sitting behind it who slowly pulled the screen back and forth while spraying it with water—shades of nineteenth-century colonial India.

During the first year of my assignment, my assistant, a woman who had long experience with the agency, decided to get married and despite the fact that her spouse was an American, she was forced to resign. For the remainder of my tour no replacement appeared and I had to do all the secret coding and type all my reports to the ambassador and the political section. Being an agency employee, I was not permitted to send messages through the Embassy code room, where coding was done mechanically. Coding was a laborious job, using code pads and what were called triads, combinations of unrelated letters, and all cable messages to and from Washington had to be coded and stamped secret.

It is usual for an American Embassy to hold a grand reception on Independence Day, but because the weather in July is insufferable, either monsoon or the start of the hot season, the reception in Delhi is held in late February, on what is now known as Presidents Day. On the last of these celebrations before he retired, Ambassador Loy Henderson decided to hold it on the lawn of his residence (officially known as the Embassy, while what is called the Embassy is officially known as the Chancery), which was a grassy area of about three-quarters of an acre surrounded by a low wall and assorted shrubbery. It was just across the street from the Chancery in a quiet residential area. Invitations were sent to the President Rajendra Prasad, to Prime Minister Jawaharlal Nehru, cabinet ministers, and senior members of the diplomatic community, as well as most Americans living in the area, all together totaling about 250 or more people.

Ambassador Henderson had, during the early post–World War I period, been the director of American relief to the Soviet Union. While serving there he had met and married a Russian woman. He had joined the Foreign Service and been assigned to a variety of posts, finally as Ambassador to the last few Embassies, and New Delhi was to be his last. Those of us junior officers hardly knew him or his wife socially, as we socialized on a different level, and as she spoke only broken English, she kept pretty much to herself.

As mentioned above, because of the severe summer weather in New Delhi the celebration of the American Independence festivities was rescheduled to a date in early spring. Several days before the event was to take place, as security officer, I was called into the Ambassador's office and introduced to several members of the Indian secret service and told to accompany them as they surveyed the grounds where the reception was to take place. This seemed the obvious thing to do, considering the prominence of the guests including the President and the Prime Minister. I watched as they climbed walls and poked about the bushes, and eventually appeared to be satisfied about where to place police and bodyguards. As we were leaving, the French doors of the house were flung open and Ms. Henderson, clad in a bathrobe and slippers, appeared and shouted at us angrily, demanding to know what we were up to. These angry words were addressed to me as I was the only sahib there. I explained to her that we were acting under orders from the Ambassador to secure the garden for the upcoming reception. This explanation seemed to mollify her somewhat, but did not assuage her anger completely as she muttered "but Loy never told me about a reception!" However, I was called by the Ambassador's secretary that Ms. Henderson wished to apologize for her rather brusque behavior. I have no idea if this experience, apologizing to a junior officer, is typical of the foreign service, but it did strike me as rather strange.

I was told by more experienced colleagues that a caste system does exist generally in the diplomatic corps, that the senior officers and the junior types, including secretaries and code clerks, do not attend the same social functions. This was the case during the first year I served in New Delhi. We junior types gave a continuing round of parties, usually with the same guests from our own as well as other diplomatic missions, and occasionally an Indian journalist. Furthermore we lived in a complex known as the "Taj," which was located in downtown New Delhi. Why it was called "Taj" was a mystery to us all. It had been built as a barracks for American army officers during WWII and was by no means uncomfortable. Each "apartment," and I use the term advisedly, consisted of two rooms connected by a passage that consisted of a bathroom big enough to be screened off for a kitchen for those who decided to set up housekeeping, even though there was a common dining room. There were two apartments for married officers, but none of these had children. Several of us combined our resources, using one room as a common bedroom and the other as a living and dining room. These rooms were not air conditioned but cooled by the ubiquitous "desert cooler."

I shared one of these "apartments" with an officer from the political section of the Embassy and, after his reassignment, with the deputy cultural affairs officer. I hired a "cook bearer," who applied for the position handing me a chit signed by a major in the British army stating that he could cook mutton to taste like chicken, beef, or pork. After hiring him I found that he was able to cook chicken, pork, or beef to taste like mutton. He also raided my liquor supply and would top up each drink he took with water to bring the level of Scotch to the level I had previously indicated. It was in this abode that I first entertained a young American woman who had come to India from London to undertake research for her doctoral thesis on the Indian elections. In one respect, I was unique. In Washington in anticipation of being assigned abroad, I was allocated a car that was shipped to me in New Delhi. Most junior foreign service officers do not have their own vehicles and have to depend on the Embassy motor pool. I was looked upon with considerable envy, but everyone knew that I was not the usual FSO. In other words, my cover was blown as soon I arrived at my new post.

I always felt that my cover was immaterial to my job, as my principal source of information was the Indian government, namely the Central Intelligence Bureau (CIB). I maintained weekly contact with the deputy director with my visits to his home in what were called the "civil lines" in the New Delhi cantonment (nomenclature continuing from the British period; after all India had been free of British rule for only four years). We were comfortable with each other and exchanged information from our respective institutions. I got much the better of the exchange, for he provided a great deal of information on the activities of the Communist Party of India (CPI) that was not otherwise available, while the activities of Americans in India were somewhat limited in those days. When I offered to compensate him for the invaluable intelligence he provided, he refused any funds or goods, but did request that I order for him a striped seersucker suit from a tailor in Baltimore. Ordering this through diplomatic channels proved to be no problem, but I never saw him wearing the suit, as he wore Indian garb whenever we met.

Other contacts that I had were called "agents" and I was their "case officer"; they worked in universities, research institutions, and as an independent journalist. I was able to set up a small think-tank consisting of one aspiring university professor and a budding young journalist. Another source was an American who piloted the private plane of a Maharaja in northeast India. A useful source, with whom I had regular contact as the Embassy security officer, was the chief of the Delhi police intelligence, who vetted Indians who were being sent to the United States on various exchange and educational programs sponsored by the U.S. government or who were about to be employed by the embassy. Police reports were not useful intelligence to me and my mission but were important to the Embassy.

The high point of my professional role in New Delhi occurred after I had been in India for about three years. During 1951 and 1952, the Chinese People's Liberation Army had swept into Xinjiang, which in theory had always been a province of China but was largely ignored by the Nationalist Government, which had recently been forced to move to Taiwan. Some of the provincial leaders, having long since agitated for independence, feared imprisonment or even death from the Communists, and so they went into voluntary exile by leading a band of Uighurs, Kazakhs, and Kyrgyz over the Karakoram Pass into Kashmir. In this effort they were promised assistance to get to Turkey by my counterpart in the U.S. Consulate in Urumchi. This band

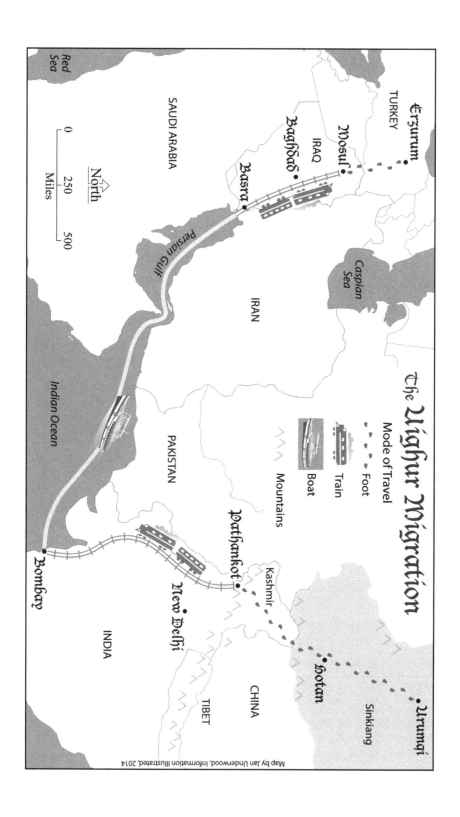

The Uighur Migration

Mode of Travel
• • • Foot
🚂 Train
🚢 Boat

∧∧∧ Mountains

TURKEY
Erzurum
Mosul
IRAQ
Baghdad
Basra
SAUDI ARABIA
Red Sea

North
Miles
0   250   500

Persian Gulf
Caspian Sea
IRAN
Indian Ocean

PAKISTAN
Pathankot
Kashmir
Bombay
New Delhi
INDIA
TIBET
CHINA
Hotan
Sinkiang
Urumqi

Map by Jan Underwood, Information Illustrated, 2014

of exiles walked some 1,000 miles across the Taklamakan desert to the Indian border, over the 12,500 foot Karakoram Pass, and into the Ladakh area of Kashmir. But an unfortunate occurrence happened while this trek was taking place: my counterpart who was to appear unidentified in India to further implement the project, took a different route, through Tibet, and was shot and killed along the way, so I was assigned to take over.

The Indian government wanted them to move on, as the already poverty-stricken state could not accommodate a sudden influx of 1,200 refugees. The CIA decided that to gain some useful future allies, either as intelligence gatherers or as propaganda broadcasters to persons remaining in liberated Xinjiang, it would help them get to eastern Turkey and I now was to be the travel agent since I was the only member of the embassy who could communicate with them. The two leaders, Muhammad Amin Bughra, formerly deputy governor of Xinjiang, and Isa Yusuf Alptekin, who led the Xinjiang independence movement, spoke some Chinese, and my knowledge of the language did come in handy. These tribal groups, along with their cousins in what used to be the former Soviet Union republics, speak a form of Turkish and the government of Turkey was willing to take them. So the exodus began: by train from Pathankot, on the Punjab-Kashmir border to Bombay, thence by pilgrim ship to Basra, then by train again to Mosul. From there they had to walk through the Kurdish region to their new homes. Walking long distances was no problem to these hardy souls, as most had been goatherds in their homelands. I never knew what became of them, but many years later I heard of a man with the name of Alptekin making anti-Chinese broadcasts from Almaty in Kazakhstan.

About a year after I arrived in New Delhi, I was approached by a very distinguished Indian woman who offered to rent the pavilion of her home for a modest sum. Her home, located in one of the finest residential areas in New Delhi, was surrounded by a beautifully landscaped garden. I leapt at the chance, glad to be away from the rather confining atmosphere of the "Taj." What's more I could meet my various contacts without their being made uncomfortable by the presence of a lot of Americans. The pavilion was semi-detached and consisted of two rooms, a bath, and a room in the servants' quarters for the bearer. By this time I had run through two of these types, and was needing a replacement. This took a bit of time as I had learned to check their "chits," references, before a short trial period. I finally found a stout Punjabi, who said his name was Shaji, and despite being a vegetarian turned out to be quite good at the job. Furthermore, he came with a small boy, I assumed a son or grandson, who swept up both in- and outdoors.

The Embassy had a softball team of sorts. We played pick-up ball on the embassy grounds; there was plenty of room, but we lacked a real opponent, since most Brits and Indians played cricket, and had little interest in "that American sport." However, once a year we played the team from the American Embassy, Pakistan, which in those days was located in Karachi. The game was played in Delhi on alternate years, and in 1951 was in Pakistan. The only means of transport was by air, and each embassy had a plane, provided by the Air Force Attaché. The New Delhi Embassy used an ancient B-17 that had been converted from a WWII bomber to a passenger plane of sorts. Fortunately the ride to Karachi was mercifully brief; anything further would have been hard on the body, as the seating was primitive to say the least. I have no recollection as to how the game went, but the first pitch to start the game off was thrown by Pakistan's first lady, Begum Liaquat Ali Khan. The pitch didn't travel very far, but was captured by several news photographers. The pictures that appeared in the newspapers on the following morning shocked the local readers, as it showed Begum Liaquat Ali Khan with her arm raised to throw the ball and a large sign behind her saying "HAMBURGERS 2 RUPEES." Pakistanis, being good Muslims, regard hamburgers as being made from ham and hence a forbidden food.

In 1951 President Truman appointed Chester Bowles for his first of two tours as Ambassador to India; President Kennedy appointed him for the second. He was an unconventional type of appointee: he and his wife, Steb, sent their children to local Indian schools rather than to the Woodstock International School in Mussoorie in the foothills. Furthermore, they were unwilling to live in the rambling structure across the street from the Chancery that housed his predecessors, which he ordered divided into several apartments for junior officers. Instead he moved into a much more modern house, recently vacated by the reassigned Deputy Chief of Mission (DCM). The house was very comfortable and there was enough room for his family, wife, and two children, and a study where he could work when he was not physically required to be at the Chancery. Working at home required a secure environment and it was up to me, as security officer, to make it so. I spent considerable time supervising the installation of safes and alarms and to make sure the place was free of taps and other listening devices. My sources in the CIB assured me that there were no such items in the house, but State Department security regulations required me to do the job. In the process, I poked around the house and came to know Chet and Steb and the family quite well. In the long run, being the mission security officer was a more useful assignment than political officer. The responsibilities were minimal and the position provided me with a reason for contact with a variety of Indian officials not available to others.

Bowles's assignment spanned the period prior to the death of Stalin and the rise of McCarthyism in the United States, and the effort to keep communism from spreading across the globe was getting into high gear. Furthermore, the new People's Republic of China was still in an alliance with the Soviet Union, which was considered potentially very dangerous. My job was to get information on left-wing activities within India and the extent to which they were penetrated by the Chinese. Congress Party, led by Nehru, dominated Indian politics in those days, and the Communist Party of India (CPI) was splintered into three separate groups: a moderate anti-Soviet party led by M. N. Roy, more a socialist than an orthodox communist; S. A. Dange, a Bombay labor leader and doctrinaire Marxist; and Jyoti Basu, the most committed, but whose efforts were largely restricted to the state of West Bengal. Throughout, Bowles took the position that rather than trying to contain the spread of communism and making it more extreme, the United States should try to understand the Eurasian dynamic and to drive a wedge between the two principals. He later set out his views in his book, *Ambassador's Report*. Since he was close to Nehru at the time, he may have influenced Nehru to take a principal role in the "Third World": a movement separate from the "First," composed of the West, and the "Second," consisting of Russia and China. His opinions did not attract much support from Truman, and when the Eisenhower administration came in with John Foster Dulles as Secretary of State, these views were considered unpatriotic. By this time, I had moved on from foreign service and "intelligence gathering," and Bowles had returned to private law practice in Connecticut. I always had great affection for Steb Bowles, the Ambassador's wife, a very charming and sensitive woman immensely popular with Indians, and a woman who was to play a very important role in my immediate future.

As previously mentioned, I was never really accepted by the other junior officers of the Embassy, or for that matter, any officer. The Ambassador found me useful. I had my own car, a gray Chevrolet, and only senior officers had black cars assigned to them from the Embassy motor pool. I was able to absent myself from the Embassy without having to justify my absence. I had money for paying my sources, whereas the others in the political section had none or had to spend much time and paperwork justifying what they might need for gathering information. Most important, I had my own abode where I could meet and entertain people without surveillance by the Embassy security service, since I was that service. This was my idyllic life until the whole structure caved in.

ME WITH MY FATHER

MY FIRST BICYCLE

ME AS A BOY

1925: MY MOTHER, MY FATHER, AND ME IN THE CAR
THAT MY FATHER DROVE TO WORK IN SHANGHAI

MY SISTER BETTY, ME, MY FATHER, MY MOTHER, AND MY
UNCLE IN FRONT OF OUR HOUSE IN SHANGHAI

ME, MY FATHER, AND MY MOTHER

AT MY PARENTS' HOME IN SHEFFIELD, MASSACHUSETTS,
AFTER SERVING IN JAPAN, ABOUT 1948

SOOCHOW CREEK FROM MY BEDROOM IN SHANGHAI

ME, MY MOTHER, AND MY FATHER ON THE FRONT
PORCH OF OUR HOME IN SHANGHAI

VIEW OF THE BUND

VIEW OF A CLOCKTOWER AT ST. JOHN'S UNIVERSITY IN SHANGHAI

CHAPTER FOUR

A New Life

𝒯HE MOST IMPORTANT EVENT OF MY LIFE TOOK PLACE in New Delhi: my encounter with Irene Tinker, a graduate student from the London School of Economics and Political Science (LSE) who drove from London to New Delhi to conduct research on India's first general election for her doctoral thesis. She owned one third of the car and had to pay off the other owners who had driven out with her and who were returning to London shortly. Furthermore the car had a "carnet de passage" that allowed the car into India without paying duty, which came to about 100% of the value of the car unless the car was sold to someone with diplomatic immunity. Well. I qualified on both counts, so I became the two-thirds owner of a Ford Anglia, vintage 1949. She held on to the remaining third. The account of her trip through Europe and the Middle East is best left for her autobiography.

Irene was expecting a job once she reached India to support her while doing her research, but found that any employment initiated in India would receive an Indian salary, so the obvious solution was some sort of liaison with someone already employed on an expatriate's salary. I decided that marriage was the obvious solution and that I would propose when she returned from her field research. In the meantime she toured much of India: Travancore-Cochin (the present Kerala), Maharashtra, Uttar Pradesh and Jammu/Kashmir. The last province was Himachal Pradesh, where it was agreed that I would meet her and drive her back to Delhi. The Indian elections of that period were staggered from state to state; very convenient for her as she could observe the polling in a variety of states over a period of two months.

The trip to Narkanda in Himachal Pradesh was complicated by the wife of the ambassador, Steb Bowles, inviting me to Thanksgiving dinner. Getting uninvited under the circumstances was a very delicate procedure. In the foreign service, one never turns down an invitation from a superior, especially one from the "first lady." When I told her that I was going to propose marriage to this woman doing research on the Indian elections, she graciously but enthusiastically told me to get on with it and not to take "no" for an answer. I drove to Narkanda, which is a small town at the end of the road, beyond which are only trails into the heart of the Himalayas. The evening after my arrival and after the polls had closed, I proposed. Irene must have thought about the proposition for a period, perhaps fifteen minutes, and accepted. We spent the night on the floor of the Dak bungalow wrapped in our sleeping bags. Also in the room (accommodations were scarce) was the BBC correspondent and the regional agent of the Congress Party, who was working on behalf of the local candidate, Rajkumari Amrit Kaur.

On our return to New Delhi, we began to make wedding plans. We could not expect members of our respective families to fly out for the wedding, so we asked local friends to help arrange the ceremony. Meanwhile, Irene had a couple of other elections to cover including the Municipality of New Delhi and would be out of town for periods in December 1951. We chose early February for the date: flowers would be out and the weather delightful.

Meanwhile back at the Embassy, I had a couple of strange experiences. I was called into the office of the DCM, who reported to me that he had been approached by the candidate from Himachal Pradesh, who claimed that I had been in her constituency handing our large amounts of money (six crores, 60,000 rupees) to the right-wing candidate and that she insisted on an accounting. I recounted my experience in the state and the fact that I had gone there to propose marriage. I think that I convinced him that I was innocent of the charge and I believe he so reported to the Rajkumari. About one week later the Ambassador called me in, having heard the same account from the Foreign Secretary, who reportedly threatened to declare me persona non grata and toss me out of India. I related the same story to the Ambassador, and like the DCM, he chose to believe it. There was no further word from the Indian government and I assumed that the episode was concluded. A few days later the Bombay scandal sheet, *Blitz*, ran a full-page, back-page story as to how an embassy officer had made large payments to right-wing candidates in Himachal Pradesh and that the Foreign Office had demanded that this person be ejected from the country. There was one hitch to the story, namely that the officer involved was the other Walker, the consul, a man who never left the city, whose only travel was between his home and the office in the Embassy. Another irony appeared in the same issue: a front-page picture of Irene at a dinner party seated between the editor of *Blitz* and the chief of staff of the Indian Army.

Considering the unusual nature of our courtship, our wedding, in early February of 1952, was decidedly traditional, held in the New Delhi Anglican cathedral with an English vicar doing the honors. We opted for the red carpet, which came to an additional twenty-five rupees. The congregation was a combination of official expatriates, several foreign newspaper reporters, and Indians, some of whom had never attended a Christian wedding or ever been inside of a church. Since there were no members of either of our families in attendance, we recruited alternatives. Irene's "father" was the BBC correspondent who had been with us in Himachal, and her matron of honor was an Indian woman, wife of one of Delhi's most prominent journalists, who at one time tried to tutor Irene in Hindi. This was a somewhat futile effort as English was widespread in India in those days, and once one left the northern part of the country, Hindi was of little use.

For our honeymoon we went back up into the foothills of the Himalayas to enjoy the crisp cold weather of the season. Few members of the Embassy seemed to be interested in travel around the country except for the more popular tourist spots such as Agra, Jaipur, and Kashmir, or to the hill stations in the heat of the summer. We were the exceptions, visiting Nepal, Darjeeling, Assam, Udaipur, and Mount Abu among others. We had planned to tour south India but my subsequent bout with hepatitis curtailed much of that other than the caves at Ellora and Ajanta.

My assignment in India was to last for another year. My personal life was as blissful and satisfying as it possibly could be, but my official life was becoming increasingly uncomfortable. For the previous year I had been acting chief of station, a position for which I had no assistance. There was in the Embassy another one of "big brother's" operatives, but he worked for another branch of the agency and I was not supposed to acknowledge any official connection. He had no assistance either but didn't have the cable traffic that I had and had only one questionable agent to handle. There was no respite to the cable traffic, which consumed most of my time in the office.

During the eight months or so that I was the sole CIA intelligence type in the Embassy, I managed to do a fair amount of traveling, particularly in north India. One advantage I had over my colleagues in the Embassy was that I had a personal car assigned to me by my employers. This meant that I could use it for pleasure as well, as though I actually owned it. At the time we had two cars, my 1949 Chevrolet and Irene's Ford Anglia. We obviously were the envy of our colleagues. This allowed us to take trips without borrowing cars and drivers from the Embassy. We took trips to Agra and Jaipur and a long one to Assam along the historic Trunk Road that linked Delhi and Calcutta. This route took us through Allahabad and Benares, but came to an abrupt end in the town of Bhagalpur in Bihar, on the banks of the Ganges. I am using the place names that were current at the time; many have been subsequently changed.

To get a vehicle across the Ganges in eastern Bihar, it was necessary to hire a railroad flatcar on which to mount the auto and attach this to a passing freight train using the rail bridge to upper Bengal and Sikkim. We had previously negotiated it with some difficulty and expected to cross in a day or two. After several days of waiting we were told that the flatcar had been expropriated by the Maharaja of Cooch Behar for his personal limousine. Our alternative was to make the rest of our trip by public transport, which actually was much more interesting. We took the third-class express, riding in the railcar with the traveling food peddlers and their cakes of ice, from Bhagalpur to Siliguri, and the famous narrow-gauge train up the escarpment to Darjeeling. We spent several days in that resort, including a day trip to Kalimpong, the door to Tibet, and a trek partway to the base of Mount Kanchenjunga. From Darjeeling we boarded a stretched Land Rover along with six other travelers for a scary trip on a one-lane twisty road to Kalimpong, a typical middle Himalayan town, and thence to Gauhati, Shillong and finally to Imphal in the state of Manipur, the most easterly town in India, each leg of the trip by train, bus, or even taxi. The bus ride to and from Shillong was particularly enchanting as young female tea pickers sang haunting local songs. Not far from Shillong is the town of Cherrapunji, which is noted as the rainiest in the world.

Such modes of transport bring one into contact with all sorts of Indians, and they seemed eager to communicate with the foreigner who in those days was rarely seen using it. From Imphal we flew to Calcutta, where we were entertained by my counterpart in the Consulate General at a notable Chinese restaurant. Once on the train back to Bhagalpur to pick up our car, I came down with a severe case of diarrhea. Our best strategy was to get back to New Delhi as quickly as possible, which meant driving nonstop. Our only accident was to hit a chicken crossing the road, but we didn't stop to confront the owner. By alternating driving, we made good time and I was able to get home to my Kaopectate without too much unpleasantness.

At some point before we were married, possibly January of 1952, the "mission" (meaning me) was visited by Evron Kirkpatrick, the Assistant Director of the Office of Special Operations, one of the top three or four senior officials from Washington. He sounded very pleased by my performance in Delhi and impressed by Irene's accomplishments, and suggested that we think about an assignment in Hong Kong. At that point I thought my future in the CIA was assured, but tragically on his return to Washington he contracted polio, was partially paralyzed, and retired from the agency. I was soon to find out that his opinion of us was not shared by those in Washington at the same level.

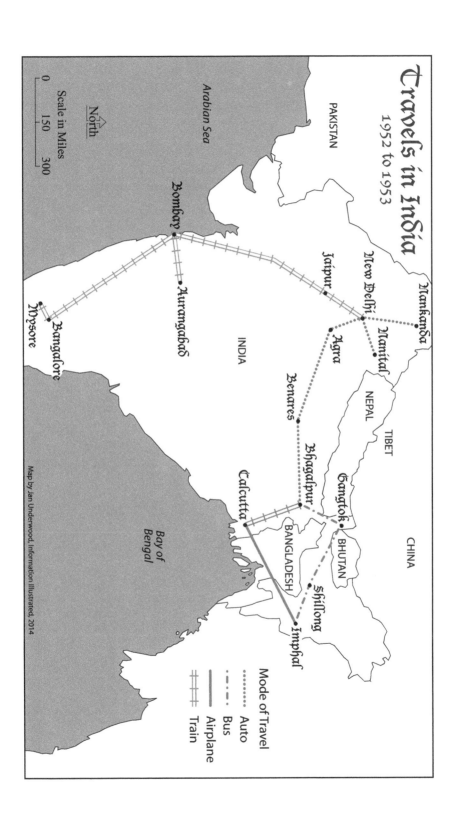

The crowning blow came when a permanent chief of station, first name Henry (I can't remember his last name; his father had been a silk merchant in Hong Kong), was assigned to New Delhi along with another special agent to assist him, so that I became number three in the pecking order. The first indignity I experienced was when the new chief insisted that I turn over to him all my contacts, which I did, except for the one in the CIB who refused to see my new boss. He was providing more intelligence than all the others put together, to Henry's embarrassment. I never knew if he actually met my contacts or whether he just glanced at the files. I immediately told these contacts that they were to report to a different case officer, which they were most reluctant to do. He forthwith demanded that I take back all the contacts, who found these acts to be entirely unprofessional, and I told Henry that I thought so as well. He cabled back to Washington that I was insubordinate, which I was, and recommended that I be removed from the New Delhi post and that I be separated from the service. I avoided Henry for the last few weeks of my tour of duty and began to make plans for my post-termination life. He appropriated the Chevrolet, but we still had the Anglia, which I agreed to sell to Henry's subordinate when we left New Delhi.

On the assumption that my career with the CIA was soon to end, Irene and I began to make plans for our return: first to England, so she could complete her doctoral program at LSE, after which I could start mine at the University of California Berkeley. Cal was selected because she had been offered a position with the Modern India Project on the Berkeley campus. Planning was complex and rather intense. We were to drive to South India, spending some time in Maharashtra at the caves in Ellora and Ajanta, spend a few days in Bombay, thence to Hyderabad and Bangalore to see the sites of the Chola dynasty, Mysore to visit the palaces, in what is now called Kerala, but the night before we were to take off I came down with a fever that was diagnosed as infectious hepatitis. This meant a delay of more than two months during much of which time I was in bed taking large amounts of fructose (or was it lactose?).

The day I came down with the fever we had to vacate our apartment, as it had been promised to a U.S. Army captain in charge of the local office of the Military Air Transport Service (MATS), which was not officially affiliated with the Embassy. He had been living in a tent on the grounds of the Gymkhana Club. Fortunately, there was a temporarily vacant Embassy house less than a block away and I was able to walk to it. The Christmas season was at hand, and we had to decline the many invitations to seasonal functions given by the diplomatic community. We did have a tree, which we decorated with what fruits and flowers we could find, and the living room had a nice fireplace on which we could pin stockings.

By early 1953, close to our first anniversary, I was well enough to travel, and we had in the interim unloaded both cars, so we packed up our cans of fructose and took public transportation: trains and buses eventually to Bombay and a boat to Africa.

CHAPTER FIVE

Africa Crossing

𝒥 RENE HAD EXPRESSED A DESIRE TO DRIVE BACK TO London but not by the same route she had previously taken. What were the alternatives? She had driven out through Greece, Turkey, Iraq, Iran, Afghanistan, and Pakistan, and these countries straddled the route back. After much research, we decided to take a ship from Bombay to Mombasa (Kenya) and drive across the Sahara or down the Nile to the Mediterranean across north Africa and across the Straits of Gibraltar and through Spain. She was able to get us a reservation for June 30, 1953, on a ferry across the English Channel, so this was the date we could not miss. We had more than six months for the Africa drive. But before we were to leave India we were determined to see more of the sub-continent. We were used to train travel and found routes that took us first through Rajasthan via Jaipur and thence to Mt. Abu, a mountain sacred to the Jain sect of Hinduism, and finally to that part of India south of Bombay. This included a side trip to the extensively carved caves of Ellora and Ajanta in central Maharashtra, then to what is considered the most engrossing part of India: Mysore and the elegantly carved temples of Somnathpur, Belur, and Halebidu dating from the Chola period in Indian history, and the massive figure of the Jain deity Gomateshwara at Shravanbelagola 120 meters tall, carved from a single rock of granite. We happened to be in Mysore during Dewali and were able to view the Maharaja's palace decorated with a myriad of festive lights. This delightful sightseeing trip was constrained only slightly by my slow recovery, as I had to be very careful of my diet, avoiding the hot spicy dishes that south India is famous for.

The trip from Bombay to Mombasa was an experience in itself. Indians constitute the largest minority in Kenya, and ocean travel is the only way to visit the homeland. The majority of passengers traveled either on deck or in the open hold, and their livelihood was easy to observe. Meals were not provided so passengers cooked their own, and some brought along their own live goats and chickens to slaughter when needed.

On reaching Mombasa we found our new car, a 1953 Austin A-40 with the UK license plate "MOP 591" awaiting us. We introduced ourselves to "Bublee," an Indian term for favorite child. Preparing it complete with roof rack and seats that could be removed and replaced by a custom-made mattress would take several days, so we accepted an invitation from an employee of the U.S. Consulate to drive to Lamu, a small island off the coast of Kenya on which the Portuguese had built a fort and supply depot for ships on their way to the Indies. Lamu turned out to be a delightful spot that in recent years has become an upscale tourist resort, much more important than Arab-dominated Zanzibar. On the return trip, our host's car began to overheat, so as we boarded the ferry across the Tana River, I grasped a pail to refill the car's radiator with water. As I leaned over the side of the ferry my glasses slipped from my shirt pocket. Without thinking, I dove into the river to try to retrieve them. The boatmen, of which there must have been ten or twelve aboard, immediately raised the alarm and pulled me out, as the crocodiles had already launched themselves from the opposite bank. Realizing that there was no way I was going to recover the glasses, with help from our host, who spoke fluent Kiswahili, we notified the local police post of the loss and stipulated a reward if the glasses were found and forwarded to the Consulate. I succeeded in getting Lloyd's to replace the glasses when we got to Nairobi, as all agreed there was no chance of finding them. However a mysterious sequel followed. This event occurred in March of 1953. Irene and I did not return to the United States until July of 1954, when we were met in New York by my mother and spent a few days at her home in Poughkeepsie. Awaiting us at her house was a small parcel that arrived in the mail the same day. It contained my glasses. I tried to find out how they had been recovered, but our friend from the Mombasa Consulate had long since departed and no one else knew about the case.

We made the usual tourist stops between Mombasa and Nairobi to watch the animals at Mudanda Rock, a rocky promontory overlooking a pond where elephants, wildebeest, various antelopes, zebra ,and a host of smaller animals come to bathe and drink, and Mzima Springs, a grand place to view hippos. These spots are clustered around the base of Mount Kilimanjaro. Our route took us across the Serengeti plains during animal migrations. Nairobi was still the seat of British Kenya, but the independence movement was in full swing, and Jomo Kenyatta was on trial for treason at a remote location on Lake Rudolph. The Mau Mau resistance movement was at its peak, and the level of tension among the Europeans was palpable.

We decided that under the circumstances we should stay

in a hotel. We picked the Green Hotel, perhaps a one- or two-star establishment, filled with journalists covering the Mau Mau uprising. We had an introduction to a Mr. Desai, who was a well-known Indian businessman with connections to the Asian community in Nairobi. We found these quite useful, as Indian lawyers were part of Kenyatta's defense team and this was an entrée to the young African intellectuals and the Ismailis as well. This latter group was prominent in Kenya, as the Aga Khan had contributed heavily to schools and colleges. We were taken to a technical college funded by the Aga Khan foundation that had recently been dedicated by Ali Kahn, the son and heir apparent, who had recently married Rita Hayworth. At the dedication ceremony, Ali and Rita were seated on two chairs on the stage of the auditorium. When the ceremony concluded and the principals rose to leave, Rita's chair rose with her, proving that American glamour girls are shaped differently from most Africans.

From the journalists at Green's we got the impression that the Mau Mau, consisting mainly of young Kikuyu males, were getting increasingly aggressive and were killing "loyal Kikuyu" at an alarming rate. Loyal Kikuyu were those who worked on British estates, or for the colonial government, or British businesses, or in some way were associated with the white establishment. Very few whites had been killed by the Mau Mau, but large numbers of Africans had, and in some cases entire villages had been wiped out by spear- and machete-wielding warriors. We decided it was best to leave Nairobi and head west toward Uganda and what was then called Belgian Congo to see if we could find a route across the Sahara. Maps showed roads from Stanleyville to Kano in Nigeria, but these were very primitive and had been drawn before the war. There had been skirmishes between the Germans on the one hand and the Free French and British on the other, and no attempt had been made to refurbish these roads in the past ten years. We were advised not to attempt them, but rather to take the route down the Nile. This meant going back to Nairobi as a starting point.

We did spend some time touring Uganda, Rwanda-Burundi, and the Belgian Congo, admiring the lakes and the Rwenzori mountain range. Although neither of us has aspirations toward big game hunting, we saw plenty of game, even close to the highway. We tried to visit a pygmy village but we were unsuccessful until we encountered some Belgian missionaries who told us to stop at any shop along the road and say "bambuti iku wapi," which was the Kiswahili for "where are the pygmies?" Following this advice we were led into the bush for about a mile and a half to a village where a primitive dance was performed for us by a group of short Africans. Apparently in this area of Belgian Congo there had been some intermarriage and pygmies were not as short as they used to be. In any event, after the dance we were asked for 200 francs, much more than the dance was worth. The pygmy villages are informally attached to the roadside shops where they trade for condiments and a few other necessities.

One of the most spectacular natural sights in this part of Africa is the Murchison Falls, where the Nile on its way from Lake Victoria spills into Lake Albert at the port of Butiaba. In 1953 there was only a jeepable road to the falls, although nowadays it is a well-visited tourist attraction. The district seat in that part of Uganda is Masindi, where we were told we might be able to rent a boat to get to the falls. Even with the help of the district officer, we were unable find a launch, all of which were in use by one or another office of the district administration. Finally someone mentioned a boat that might be available in Butiaba. We drove to Butiaba and to our dismay the boat in question was the *African Queen*, the same vessel used by Humphrey Bogart and Katharine Hepburn in the film of the same name. It would be nice to say that we took the *African Queen* to Murchison Falls, but the harbormaster insisted that the boat was not seaworthy and he would not permit it to leave port. Thus we missed one of the major natural wonders of Africa.

To learn more about possible routes north, we felt that it was important to return to Nairobi, which was on the major north-south axis of Africa. Information was forthcoming, none of it very encouraging. A couple who had driven a VW bug south from Addis Ababa had broken down in the Ethiopian highlands and waited a month for a replacement axle and finally gave up and rode a truck the rest of the way. Under no circumstances would they recommend that route. Another possibility was to go north along the rift valley, meet up with the Nile, and take a boat to Juba in the Sudan and thence by road to Khartoum. These roads had not been maintained and would be very difficult if not impossible for a car such as Bublee. Finally several old East Africa hands mentioned the route around the horn of Africa: through Somalia, which was administered by the UN; British Somaliland, which had not yet become independent; thence to Addis via Hargesia; to Eritrea and to Khartoum. This seemed to be a long way around to get to Cairo, but the consensus among the cognoscenti was that it would be negotiable. Meanwhile, we were beginning to get a bit antsy about further touring in Kenya. On our way back from Uganda we passed within three miles of the town of Lari at the time that the Mau Mau were slaughtering 400 loyal Kikuyu, the deadliest of the killings to date, an act that brought down the might of the British armed forces on Mau Mau strongholds on Mount Meru. As a matter of fact we had even seen their encampments when we visited an LSE classmate of Irene's who was the district officer of that area. Get under way was the bottom line.

The road from Nairobi to the Somali border was not difficult, and once we got out of range of the Mau Mau we began to enjoy the trip. Garissa, on the banks of the Tana River, was our first objective. This was the territory of the Wakamba, a lowland tribe who distrusted the upland Kikuyu and sought succor from the British. We spent a couple of days in Garissa during which the game warden took us crocodile hunting. Months later he mailed one of the properly tanned skins of an animal that I had shot.

As we headed eastward toward the border, the roads deteriorated but were still passable as long as it didn't rain. Liboi is the name of the border post manned by a single African who did not know if he was a Kenyan or a citizen of Somalia. He merely identified himself as a Somali, and it was unclear which jurisdiction he worked for. He kept records in a student's copy book, was embarrassed by his unfamiliarity with written English, and had me fill out the information of our crossing in his record book. I noticed that there had been eight crossings both ways across the border since the beginning of the year and five of these had been the UN locust eradication service. So he did not lead a busy life.

As we left the border, we ran into a light drizzle that slowed our going but was not enough to get us stuck. It began to become dark and the road was difficult to follow, but as we made it up a slight rise to the top of a low ridge, we saw the ocean and a blaze of lights! It seemed like a mirage. We had not encountered a single soul since leaving Liboi. This had to be Kismayo, the major town of southeast Somalia. We drove to the beach and, too tired for anything but sleep, we unrolled out sleeping bags and sacked out. When we awoke next morning we were surrounded by forty to fifty curious Somalis who watched as we struggled into our clothes inside our sleeping bags. Actually, the dazzling display of lights we had seen the night before came not from the town but from a cruise ship anchored offshore. Our immediate requirement was petrol and we needed local cash to pay for it. Our U.S.

dollars were unfamiliar to local merchants, but we found the municipal office, which was still staffed by Italians who were only too pleased to convert our currency to lira.

We were eager to move on, so as soon as we gassed up we took off for Mogadishu for we feared we might run into more rain if we tarried. The land between the two coastal towns is lush, and the Italians who had colonized the country had converted it to growing luscious fruit crops. Some of the world's best grapefruit comes from Somalia. The Italians had spent considerable resources on Mogadishu, with broad avenues along the waterfront lined with palms and what must have been handsome resort hotels. The UN had retained many of the former Italian municipal employees and, unlike many of the other African countries seeking self-determination, there was no obvious anti-colonial movement. None of the tribal friction that broke out three decades later was obvious during out visit, and we enjoyed a restful few days before venturing across the Ogaden.

Crossing the Ogaden—the desert region lying in the eastern portion of Ethiopia—was a unique experience for us. In those days there was no real road, only a track used mainly by prospectors of the Sinclair Oil Company. We had been told in Mogadishu that there was a Sinclair encampment about halfway across the Ogaden where we could find water and a secure place to spend the night. After a full day's drive from Fer-fer on the Somali border we found the camp without difficulty and were heartily welcomed by its personnel, most of whom were American geologists. Of course they were most curious about us and our little sedan, for they drove around in Dodge Power Wagons. They expressed some skepticism about the Austin's ability for the next piece across the desert because there was a slight slope that made the going a lot tougher.

Nevertheless, the next morning with a full supply of

water we took off for Wardheer, the only town along the way to our next objective, Awareh, which was a district seat in the former colony of British Somaliland. The slight slope was definitely a problem and we were repeatedly stuck in the fine sand. We did carry two metal tracks, each about three feet long, which we could place in front of the rear wheels to provide purchase to enable us to get going again. However, once under way, the driver, usually Irene, had to stop to allow me—who had to retrieve the tracks—to rejoin the expedition. This happened two or three times, the car getting restuck each time it slowed, and my getting increasingly tired, so we agreed that she would not stop until she came to the top of the rise or reached more solid ground. An added incentive to move along was supplied by a covey of buzzards circling above the acacia tree under which I was sitting drinking my hepatitis concoction. Well, I found myself walking about two and a half miles in over 100-degree heat and loose sand before I finally caught up to her. The track improved marginally but not enough that we felt confident about stopping under any circumstances.

When we reached Wardheer we drove right through town much to the consternation of the local police, who took umbrage by firing a few rounds at the speeding car. We had expected to reach Awareh before nightfall, but our bout with the sand had slowed us down and we drove the last twenty-five or thirty miles after dark. Awareh was actually in Ethiopia, but since the end of World War II the region along the Ethiopian–British Somaliland border had been administered by the British as the Ethiopians had consented to foreign assistance in establishing law and order for years since the defeat of the Italians. We were somewhat concerned at having to dodge large collections of what looked like tumbleweed and which we were told were used as barriers by "shiftas," local tribesmen, who were goatherds during the day and highwaymen at night. Fortunately the only being we saw on that portion of the route was a lion, caught up in our headlights. We were told that unlike most African lions, males inhabiting the horn do not have manes and from a distance are indistinguishable from females. This lion, regardless of sex, slowed us down but otherwise gave us no trouble.

It must have been about eight o'clock when we reached the district headquarters in Awareh. We found the district officer's home dark and unoccupied, but nearby was a large tent ablaze with lanterns and candles. We crept up to the tent only to find that the assistant D.O. in full dress having dinner with his wife. The look of astonishment on his face when he saw us at the tent flap and heard us speaking American English was impossible to describe. When he learned we had come across the Ogaden he turned ashen, blurting out that his superior, the D.O., had been killed by shiftas that very day, which explained why the house was unoccupied. He graciously offered to put us up in the D.O's empty house. Actually we slept quite well that night and the A.D.O. fed us a hearty breakfast the next morning.

Our next objective was Hargeisa, the capital of British Somaliland. Britain had not started the process of granting independence to its African colonies, so British administrative services were still ensconced in that territory. We were to join up with an Italian employee of Sinclair driving a pickup truck who would escort us through Jigjiga and Harar as far as Dire Dawa and see that we got past official and ad hoc customs posts. These "customs posts" were located throughout Ethiopia to collect "passage money" from travelers. Our Italian benefactor, who traveled this route regularly and was fluent in most of the local languages, including Amhara, was able to talk our way past these posts without undue delay. Whether he or Sinclair had a long-term arrangement with these "customs agents" we never knew, but we paid no "passage money." We later learned from personnel at the U.S. Embassy in Addis Ababa that even a diplomatic passport or license plate on the vehicle would not get you past these posts without coughing up some "bakshish."

Harar is a striking city, perhaps the second most important in Ethiopia. It is the easternmost town of the western plain and a cultural center for the Danakil people. It is an old city with narrow streets running through residential areas with high mud walls on each side. The people are mostly Muslim and their orientation is more toward the Red Sea and the Arabian peninsula. Dire Dawa is on the Franco-Ethiopian railway, which runs from Addis to Djibouti, and was the principal land connection that Ethiopia had with the outside world. We found to our chagrin that the availability of this rail line meant that the roads built during the war had been neglected.

For fourteen miles out of Dire Dawa the road was in very good condition, since it led to a shrine that was frequented by the Emperor Haile Selassie. Beyond this the road deteriorated rapidly and in many cases we had to rebuild it ourselves. In its operative days Irish bridges had been built across the small rivers that flowed down from the hills, but these too were broken up through lack of maintenance. In one instance we had to drain a pond to make sure that the water was not too deep for Bublee to get through. The first evening as we were trying to push the car up a bank from a dry streambed, we heard a faint roar from upstream to which we paid little attention as we thought a train was approaching; the railroad was not that far away. But suddenly we realized that the sound came from the north while the railroad was to the south; it was the rush of water down the stream, which began to rise rapidly. The car was only a third of the way up the bank and the water made the surface very slippery. Frantically we unloaded as much of the car as we could and prayed that the river would not inundate the poor car or wash it downstream. The water rose only as high as the rear wheel wells. Thankful that we and the car had survived, we pushed the car up the slope and retired for the night, sleeping in the car.

Apparently in the foothills there is little rainfall, but rain at the higher elevations is not infrequent and the runoff can cause considerable damage, as we were soon to find out as we approached the Awash, the major river in the region. The streams dissipated as quickly as they filled, and next morning we were able to proceed, but not very far.

Our next obstacle was the Awash River, the principal river in that part of Ethiopia. The flash flood we had encountered the day before had done considerable damage to the "Irish bridge," and a Jeep station wagon carrying some Catholic nuns had been swept several miles down the river. Fortunately the passengers had abandoned the vehicle only moments before, but we saw the remains of the Jeep in Addis and there was not a recognizable piece of the vehicle left.

The closest town was Mieso, also on the rail line, and we were told that we could load Bublee on a flatcar and be railed across the river. "When would there be a flatcar?" we asked. "Soon" was the answer. Mieso was a characterless dingy town with a single run-down hotel used primarily by prostitutes. Incidentally, an occasional Fiat 18-wheeler employed the road from Djibouti, which augmented the damage done by neglect and the weather, and it was the drivers of these trucks who patronized the women. After three miserably anxious days a flatcar finally arrived, and with Bublee aboard we reached the other side of the river in less than ten minutes. Our first encounter on the opposite bank was with the UN locust control unit. On more than one occasion we ran into these units; locusts were a major problem in East

Africa, though the control units seem to have made little progress, and in some regions in the horn of Africa and in Yemen, locusts were a special food item. The head of this unit was a well-turned-out Englishman who ended up being the only person I have ever met who fought with Franco in the Spanish civil war.

The remainder of the trip finally to Addis was uneventful. We were filthy and decided to stay at a pension in the upper part of the city rather than a hotel. We drove around the area looking for it, then finally we decided to ask for directions. We spied a parked van that I recognized as belonging to USIS (the United States Information Service), which meant there was an English speaker somewhere close. A short wait was rewarded by the appearance of a handsome young American couple, and Irene immediately recognized the husband as a classmate. Rather than give us directions to a place they did not know of, they invited us home for a bed and bath.

We stayed with them for four days while Irene with newspaper credentials from the *Statesman* in New Delhi sought an audience with the Emperor. He turned out to be a modest and not imperious personage, and his palace was the shabbiest of any we have encountered, enclosed as it was in shiny corrugated tin roofing. We were shown around the city and the bazaars and purchased some folk artwork. Our friends were so accommodating we would have liked to have stayed longer, but we were beginning to worry about time. We were hardly halfway through our trip and we had to be in Calais, France, by June 30; if we didn't make it, we would have to either wait for another opening, which was rare at that time of year, or leave the car in France and come back for it at another time.

Reluctantly we left Addis and headed due north toward Asmara in Eritrea, via Dese and Adigrat. The roads in the northern part of Ethiopia were considerably better than those we encountered in the east, and we made this leg without incident. Two things stand out in my mind about Asmara. The first was the very modern Catholic cathedral, which looked rather out of place in a poverty-stricken country still recovering from Italian colonialism and its demise after World War II. The city is rather strikingly divided into a section of tree-lined boulevards built by the Italians and the rather squalid areas of the local population.

The second was the Sudanese representative in Asmara, Mohammed Yassein, who had been at LSE with Irene and who was happy to give us letters of introduction to his colleagues in Khartoum. From Asmara we took the direct route to the Sudanese border; in retrospect, I didn't think there was an alternate, although current maps show routes heading north and west. Besides, we were headed for Khartoum via Kassala, the Sudanese town closest to the border. The inhabitants of the few villages we passed seemed more Arab than any we had seen in our trip so far, being just across the Red Sea from Saudi Arabia. The customs checkpoint was staffed by Copts, who were very unhappy about their posting in a predominantly Muslim country and showed this by giving us a hard time, making us unload everything from the roof and pawing through all our belongings. We were only grateful that they didn't dump out precious water and petrol. It was just a short drive from the border to Kassala, where we were warmly welcomed by officials from the civil service of Sudan who were colleagues of Yassein. We would have liked to have spent several days in Kassala, with better than average accommodations and friendly Sudanese officials, but we were warned that to drive across the desert to Khartoum we needed to be accompanied by a second car. Furthermore, it was too hot during the day, so you could only drive at night. We learned that the Chief of Police from Khartoum, who was visiting family in this region, was going to drive back to the capital the next evening, and we in our car could drive in tandem. This was too good a deal to pass up; none could guarantee another opportunity such as this. Reluctantly we loaded up the car, thanked our new friends, and at dusk the next day we set off to cross the desert to Khartoum.

We followed the Chief's car at some distance because of the dust, but keeping a sharp lookout for its tail lights. His driver was experienced with desert tracks and drove rather faster than we would have liked. Our trip through Ethiopia had taken us through deeper sand, and we thought more caution was needed. The tracks in the sand we followed were initially obvious, but after a couple of hours of they began to peter out. Irene was driving at this time and had noticed that about a mile back, more evident tracks had turned right (north) up a slight rise. She signaled the car ahead, and the driver agreed to back up. To his and our surprise, a short distance up this rise the tracks joined a very well-traveled set of tracks that ran east-west. We didn't follow these tracks for very long before we came to a trucker's tea stop. The driver now recognized our location, and after a glass of tea we sped on to Khartoum, arriving there as the sun rose.

Again, benefitting from Irene's LSE contacts, we were well treated in Khartoum: being put up at a nice hotel, and more importantly, having opportunities to meet with important people in the government to learn about Sudan's current political situation, and relations with Egypt and Great Britain. Irene was doing a lot of interviewing while I was looking into routes we could take north to Egypt and eventually to Cairo. There was no Nile access to Egypt as there were unnavigable rapids where the river curved north and west around the Nubian dessert. Very few of those we met in Khartoum had ever driven to Egypt. They had flown or taken the train. During World War II British colonial military had crossed the desert and marked their route with a line of intermittent oil drums on which they could triangulate their position periodically. However, many of these oil drums had been buried by frequent sandstorms. We were told it might be possible to hire a taxi to accompany us on which we could triangulate, but this would entail paying the taxi driver's fare for both directions, making the cost prohibitive. It was as though we had painted ourselves into a corner.

Irene came up with the idea of putting Bublee on a flatcar attached to one of the scheduled trains. After all, we had done this to cross the Awash in Ethiopia, but the weather was cool and the trip had lasted only an hour or two. Here the heat would be unbearable. Plenty of cars had been shipped in this fashion back and forth over the desert, but, we were told, never with occupants. We really had no alternative but to abandon the rest of the trip and sell the car in Khartoum. We were young and healthy and we had experienced hardships before. Irene had driven across desert-like terrain on her trip to India and the weather had been somewhat like that of northern Sudan. So we decided: we would drive to Abu Hamed, to the end of the road, and find a flat railroad car. However, we were told that there was no loading platform there; the only one was in Atbara, about a third of the way. The road that far was quite good and we left the car there to be loaded. Within a short time we went to the station to climb up to Bublee only to find that it had been mounted so that when the train was under way we would be riding backward. What was worse, the turbulence created by the moving train would suck up the sand and push it through any open window of the car. We would have to keep the windows closed and the situation would get worse when we started across the real desert. As the train headed north, the interior of the car became increasingly uncomfortable. We had to open the windows a slight crack but that meant we would be covered with sand. We traveled like this as far as Abu Hamed, where the train stopped. The platform was crowded with men waiting for the next passenger train. Irene got out of Bublee, dropped to the ground, and began looking for a "restroom," which the station appeared to lack. She circled the train looking for an empty box car in which she might hide, and surprisingly found at the tail end what looked like a private car. She ran up to the door and pounded on it, hoping someone would let her in. The door was opened by a man who appeared to be a servant but who barred the door. Irene's desperate pleas aroused his boss, who appeared dressed in a bathrobe, obviously wakened from his Ramadan sleep. Expressing considerable dismay at a sand and dust–encrusted foreign woman coming unannounced from nowhere, he immediately invited her to join him in his car and pointed the way to the bathroom beyond the bedroom. She relieved herself, washed up a bit, and returned to the living area. By the time I had appeared, after securing the car and locking doors and shutting windows, she was answering questions posed by our rescuer, such as why we were riding in an automobile mounted backwards on a flatcar. She was giving him an account of our travel so far and the connections that we had made in Khartoum. Many of those connections were indeed his friends and members of the Western-educated officials from the Arab elite. He was more than gracious— having his cook-bearer prepare us a meal, even though it being Ramadan he could eat none of it. As the train started up again, he gestured toward the bedroom and suggested we might like to lie down. We were a bit embarrassed, but he assured us he would be comfortable in the main section of the car. In this manner we crossed the Nubian desert and by morning we had arrived in Wadi Halfa.

We had a letter of introduction to an important local Sheikh, who welcomed us with enthusiasm. A six foot four Sudanese swathed in a white robe, his was a most impressive presence. He was the caterer for the Nile ferry line operating between Wadi Halfa and Aswan, the first town in "Upper Egypt," and his first kindness was to take us to one of the ferries and order us breakfast. He also got us a room at the local hotel and arranged passage on the next ferry for us and Bublee. After a day's leisurely sailing up the Nile to see some of the ancient sites, we were ready to move on. Bublee was on the accompanying barge and we were fortunate enough to have one of the few cabins. As I looked back on our stay in Sudan, whether it was Kassala, Khartoum, Atbara, the train, or Wadi Halfa, I am impressed by the warmth of our reception, much of it a reflection of the introduction by Yassein, Irene's friend from LSE. I also got the impression that it would have been even warmer if I hadn't been along.

Knowing that we had to make our Channel crossing on June 30, we had to move along. We off-loaded Bublee at El Shellal and headed north toward Luxor on a very rough road over hilly terrain, and Bublee began to object. Then engine began to heat up and cough so that we had to stop often to pour river water into the radiator. We finally made it to Luxor, and after a good night's sleep we left Bublee with an auto mechanic while we took a guided tour to Thebes across the river. The Valley of the Kings had not been fully cleaned up from years of neglect from the war. I was eager to see what had happened to Bublee, and upon finding the garage and the mechanic, I was told the problem was common in Egypt, as the petrol sold throughout was not highly refined but "bordering asphalt," so that the valves were having difficulty doing their job. He had cleaned the valve assembly and the car was ready. Very early the next morning we headed north along the river, through densely cultivated fields: in this region arable land extended less than a kilometer from the river. We had been urged to stop less than halfway into the trip at a place called Qena and cross the river to see Cleopatra's tomb at Dendera. We had difficulty crossing the Nile each way, as we had to use public ferries, crowded dhows to which we had to wade out to board. The tomb turned out to be very ordinary, and we were very hot, hungry, and eager to move on when we got back to our car. The remainder of the trip to Cairo went without incident, and the road, in comparison to our recent encounters, was good.

Cairo impressed us unlike any of those cities we had previously encountered, in that it was cosmopolitan and had a distinctive Mediterranean flair, with branches of European shops and chain hotels, and broad streets almost completely devoid of horse- and human-drawn carts. There was much talk of General Neguib, the presumed head of the military regime, and General Gamal Nasser, who was the real power in the council.

I have little other recollection of our stay in Cairo except for two isolated events. One was our attendance at a movie, the first ever produced with a stereopticon vision, the type for which you had to wear glasses provided by the theater to get the full stereo effect. I remember these glasses as bulky white-rimmed specs. But for me these glasses had no effect, as I could only see out of one eye. The other was an encounter with G. K. Reddy, the author of the story on the back page of *Blitz* that featured the account of a man named Walker who was dispensing large sums of money to election candidates in Himachal Pradesh and whom the Indian Foreign Office had asked to be deported, a complete fabrication, of course. When I confronted him, he offered a rather lame explanation that he was young, only just starting out as a journalist, and infused with the culture of *Blitz*. He apologized profusely and I reminded him that nothing ever came of it.

We were fortunate to meet Judge Brinton of the Anglo Egyptian Mixed Court, a feature of past colonialism. If foreigners, principally British, American, and French, get into legal problems, they are not tried in Egyptian courts but in those presided over by a judge of the foreign national involved. This practice, known as extraterritoriality, also was used in Shanghai until the Japanese took over the city.

Judge Brinton owned a villa on the Mediterranean a short distance to the west of Alexandria and suggested we spend a night or two before our drive along the North African coast. Bearing in mind our Calais-Dover deadline, we were happy to leave Cairo. Delightful as was the judge's villa, we knew we had to push on. The drive along the coast was less taxing than those we had encountered earlier, but we were warned never to leave the roads as there were still unexploded minefields, a residue from the North African campaigns of World War II that had never been systematically cleared. Names came up as we drove along the coast, names of towns often heard during the campaign: El-Alamein, Tobruk, Sidi Barrani, and we found plenty of remaining evidence of heavy fighting. As with each previous border, we anxiously approached, not knowing the setup of the facility or the professionalism of the personnel. In the case of the Egyptian-Libyan border, we had been informed that there still existed the notion that Libya consisted of two questionable nations: Cyrenaica to the east, with Benghazi as its administrative center, and Tripolitania to the west, with Tripoli as its center. As a nation Libya was in limbo; there was no person or organization within the indigenous population to take on the act of governance. We heard of nomadic tribal chiefs in Fezzan in the desert southern half of the country, but they had been largely ignored. In the northeast dwelt the Senussi, whom we encountered during the first part of our drive and from whom we heard rather critical remarks about the Fezzan, but much more critical remarks about the Italians, who had tried to combine them into a single nation.

Since Italy had lost control of its African colonies (Libya, Eritrea, Somaliland, and Ethiopia) after the war, their governance, excluding Ethiopia, which had its Emperor, was left to the United Nations and its collection of international designees, many of whom were returning Italians who resumed many of the lower-level administrative functions. The Italians tended to be monumental, as shown by remaining public structures in Mogadishu, Addis, and Asmara. The Europeans we encountered in Libya were British soldiers, some of whom had been in the North African campaign and were very helpful when Bublee needed attention.

From Derna the road veered slightly to the south, leaving the coast and heading across a hard sand and stone desert that led us to Benghazi. I have little recollection of the drive across Libya, except for the colonial efforts by the Italians: dividing up the coastal areas into regular-sized plots with modest houses into which Italian farmers would move and take up farming in an unfamiliar terrain and which were now occupied by Senussi nomads with their disorderly herds roaming the plots. We did stop to investigate the impressive Greek ruins near Barce and later in Tripolitania Roman ruins not far from Misrata. Rounding the southern tip of the Gulf of Sirte, the road deteriorated and we had to be careful to avoid the potholes that had been ignored for the past eight or more years. A few miles after El Agheila, the first town in Tripolitania, we came across a most amazing towering structure: a huge arch, Mussolini's Triumphal Arch, a recognition of his dream of creating an African branch of metropolitan Italy. We figured that there had been sufficient activity around this structure to have removed or detonated any remaining land mines, and therefore it would be safe to camp on the ground.

It was more or less an uneventful shot from the Arch to Tripoli. The road surfaces varied widely, some untouched since the war and others, unfortunately short stretches, that had been recently repaved. There was one rather significant attraction as we neared Tripoli: the partially restored Roman town of Leptis Magna, which in recent years has become a major tourist attraction.

I have little recollection of the city except that what we saw of it looked like a run-down version of a town in Italy, and that after dinner at a so-called Italian restaurant, I came down with a violent case of food poisoning with vomiting and diarrhea. The hotel room, which was part of a restored officers club, had no attached bathroom, but fortunately a bidet that served as a timely substitute. Irene was also affected, but much more mildly, and our discontent was increased by loud voices from drunken American airmen in town from the local airbase. There was little to keep us in Tripoli so the next day we set off towards Tunis, our final destination in Africa. We had expected to drive through Tunisia, Algeria, and Morocco to Tangier and then up through Spain, but we had to make the June 30 ferry. The 60-odd miles from Tripoli to the border were not difficult and based on our experience on the Egyptian side, we expected a quick passage. However to our chagrin, the border officer looking at our passports insisted there was no evidence that we had entered Tripolitania from Cyrenaica and we should go back to Tripoli and have the authorities stamp entrance permissions on our passports. We had no intention of driving back so we tried to negotiate with the guy. This proved to be difficult; he was enjoying being superior over two obvious Americans. Irene vented her anger, using demeaning language until I told her to shut up. She drove the car a short distance to shade under a tree, while I enticed the customs officer to talk to the District Officer, his superior in rank. After some discussion the DO stamped the passports and said we could now leave for the border. The DO was obviously looking for some sort of compensation, so I gave him several packs of cigarettes. We were so pleased to enter Tunisia, with its strong French presence and the best kept roads we had encountered in many miles.

This marked the termination of our African adventure. I am quite ready to admit that I relied heavily on Irene's notes, which appeared many years later in published form entitled *Crossing Centuries: A Road Trip Through Colonial Africa.* There is a story about how it took so long to appear after it was first submitted to a publisher. Here was a manuscript containing firsthand descriptions of the political and revolutionary events of the time and interviews with individuals who became important to the burgeoning history of Africa. In any event, the publisher returned the manuscript in favor of one by another young American woman who was involved in an affair with the son of the Sultan of Morocco. I insert this account because it shows how little the rest of the world cared about the end of European colonialism and the leaders who shaped modern Africa.

Tunisia appeared to us as more European, and certainly more cosmopolitan than what we experienced elsewhere on the continent. Its history encased many accounts of European incursions into its lands, from Greeks, Romans, Carthage, to Saint Augustine, to traders to invaders, to its importance as a military bastion in wars over the centuries. The drive from the border to Tunis was diverted twice. The first time was to the island of Djerba, which was inhabited by Berbers, Arabs, and a community of Jews, all of whom appeared to be living in a world of past centuries. Since the island was connected to the mainland by a causeway on which no motorized vehicle was allowed, both cultural and economic communication was difficult. It amused us to see men going around on the backs of donkeys. But crossing the English Channel kept calling, so after one night's rest in a tiny hotel room we crossed the causeway, picked up Bublee, and moved on in a northerly direction. In addition I needed some medical attention for a case of dysentery I had picked up in Tripoli.

On the last leg to Tunis our second diversion, the only memorable sight, was a well-preserved Roman coliseum in El Djem, one that was more replete than the one in Rome. Daily life, including sales of vegetables and other provisions, extended right up to the walls of the edifice. The interior looked more like a place for a game of soccer than a site for a fight between a gladiator and a lion.

Tunis seemed to be a good place to relax and plan for our return to Europe, but finding the right method proved difficult. There was a car cum passenger ferry to Palermo in Sicily, but space for Bublee was difficult to find. Eventually we and the car arrived at the ferry dock ready to board, but the customs officers demanded we unload the car and remove the items from the roof. Irene in her broken French persuaded them to leave the water bags and jerry cans attached.

I can't remember much about the drive up the boot, except for Florence. I had developed a painful lesion under my right arm that needed a doctor to lance it and apply dressings. I found out that at the consul was the same officer and his wife who had schemed with us in New Delhi to conceal the fact that Irene and I were living together before we married. He produced a doctor who did the necessary surgery, and again we were on our way north. On June 29 we arrived in Calais, presented ourselves at a small pension, and asked the woman at the front desk what she would give us by way of room and food for the small amount of change we had left. She looked us over and to our delight we got a room, a bed with clean sheets, a bathroom, and a decent meal. Next morning we were rewarded with tickets on the ferry to Dover for two adults and their car. Upon our arrival in London Irene looked at the mileage gauge on Bublee's dashboard, which said 12,918 miles from Mombasa.

LONDON TIME

We had a great time in London: nice accommodations in a B&B near North Kensington Square, close to LSE, where Irene had to spend time with faculty to finish her doctorate. We did have time to attend the theater and eat in good restaurants, because prices were still at their postwar low, as well as associate with her friends. But this had to come to a close after a few weeks, for I had to return to Washington and the CIA to settle accounts. I still had some salary coming to me, and I wanted to collect the cost of two people flying from New Delhi to Washington, but I had to be there to collect it. Since it was cheaper than flying, I crossed the Atlantic first west and then, after completing my mission, east by ship in third-class cabins. My stay in Washington lasted about six weeks, during which time I stayed with family or friends, to get some of the funds I expected. I didn't get the rest until a year later. The headquarters of the CIA was still located in Temporary 8, a tarpaper-enclosed wood building dating from WWII located on the Mall, a reflection of the low esteem and support the agency enjoyed from the Eisenhower administration.

When my return ship docked in Southampton, I was greeted by a lovely young woman wearing a hat and a beautiful orange overcoat. It took me more than a moment to realize she was my wife, for the only coats I had seen her in were unadorned outer garments you would wear on a safari, and as for hats, this one you would not wear in tropical sunshine. We drove Bublee up to London to a lovely garden apartment in the rear of a house owned by a professor from the University of London located on Highgate West Hill, not far, within a short walk, from the Highgate Northern Line tube station. Hence it was easy to get down to the center of London's theater and intellectual (universities and the British Museum) district. Since Irene was totally involved in the completion of her dissertation on the Indian elections and earning her doctorate, I decided to advance my academic life, which resulted in enrolling in the School of Oriental and African Studies to earn a master's in Chinese history. This I never accomplished as there were too many diversions: courses in South and Southeast Asia and on Africa dealing with the process of decolonialization.

For the better part of a year we luxuriated in London, making the best of the remaining post–World War II reduced prices for restaurants, theaters, and concert performances. Since we still had Bublee we were able to get around the British Isles: Scotland, Ireland, and Wales.

BACK TO AFRICA

Still having a capable car we decided in the spring of 1954 to attempt to complete the remainder of our planned drive through Africa. So after Irene received her doctorate from LSE and I an MS from SOAS, we were ready to go. Our plans were somewhat curbed by the insurrection in Algeria, where there was armed conflict between the French and the Berber nationalists. This conflict had not yet crept into Morocco primarily because the Sultan had some prominence and the French kept their distance. The French agricultural and business presence in Algeria was much more intense than that in Morocco and they were trying to hang onto it. So we, along with my mother, who had joined us in London some time earlier, were on "the Road to Morocco," via southern France, Spain, Gibraltar, and Tangier. What I recall from the European phase of this trip was a stay with some LSE friends of Irene's in Barcelona and a side trip to Andorra. This tiny kingdom, like Shanghai, admitted Jewish refugees fleeing from Nazi Germany without documentation. We encountered a man who had been in both places who struck up a conversation with my mother and emphatically called her "Madame de Shanghai."

What I remember of the trip through Spain was the contrast between rural poverty and the cathedrals where the figures in the chapels were lavished in gold. Another experience was the presence of Franco's military police, in rather formal caped black garb and three-cornered hats, along the sides of the highways waving us to slow down or to stop and be looked over. We were never detained or questioned, but this was a source of tension. Spanish towns seemed rather sleepy during the day but at night they came alive with music and food carts and friendly gathering, usually lasting until 11 or 11:30. Having come from countries with Arab mosques (India, Pakistan, East Africa), we were surprised at the number remaining in good condition in southern Spain, reminding us that Muslims were an important part of Spain's history. We hurried through Seville and the Prado and I remember a courtyard because of its name: Generalife.

Now it was on to the straits and Tangier and on south, but beginning with a detour to Tetuan in the miniature Spanish enclave of Ceuta on the Mediterranean coast. This was a delightful town where the hills came down to the sea and coves where pirates hid their lairs. We spent a night in a little B&B and to our annoyance we found that someone had broken into Bublee and taken the ammunition for my trusty revolver, which before and after I never had to use; a few weeks later as we were crossing the Atlantic, I unceremoniously threw it overboard. From the coast we headed toward the Moyen Atlas mountain range. The eventual objective was Marrakech, although there was plenty to see along the way. We had to be careful and fly our American flag, because there were episodes of hostility against the French. We heard about one tactic used by the independentists, which was to set a chicken afire and throw it into a French-owned farm field and watch it scurry about setting the crops afire.

Meknes was a typical Berber walled city dominated by a large mosque. We were able to enter the souk, which seemed to be operating normally. As usual, foreigners were not allowed to reside in the city, and accommodations were just outside the main gate. From there we drove to higher elevations through a town I seem to remember as Kasbah Tadla where the Europeans retired during the hot seasons. A pleasant drive down the mountain put us in Marrakesh, which is the best combination of Arabic and Berber culture in northwest Africa. An easy drive took us to Casablanca, which was quite a contrast: a thoroughly Europeanized commercial Atlantic port. There we put Bublee on a cargo ship bound for New York. We went north by train stopping briefly in Rabat, a sleepy town where we met the leaders of the Istiqlal, soon to form the government of the new self-governing nation of Morocco. We hurried on to Tangier and Gibraltar, where we took ship to New York. This marked the end of our African adventure, and when later both Irene and I visited Africa either together or separately, it was an entirely different continent.

At this point, I must acknowledge that most of the account of crossing Africa came from a book of the trip that Irene created from the copious notes she assembled while I drove. She was the one who interviewed those who were making the new post-colonial Africa. I attended most of these sessions, except when I was making sure that Bublee would take us to our next destination.

CHAPTER SIX

California

WE HAVE CROSSED MANY OCEANS IN OUR TIME, AND enjoyed all the crossings but this one. Lacking funds for first-class accommodations we had to settle for second, which provided sex-segregated dormitory cabins, so we spent most of the trip on deck. Our intention was that on arrival in New York we would pick up Bublee and drive to Berkeley, California, where Irene would take up the appointment promised her by Professor Dick Park, the best man at our wedding, at the Modern India project at the University of California. But we had a two-week wait until Bublee arrived in New York. Bublee had visited several other ports en route from Morocco. This allowed us to spend some time with our families, with my mother in Poughkeepsie, New York, and with Irene's in Delaware. Once Bublee arrived, we wasted no time heading due west. Irene was eager to take the Modern India job, so the only stop we made was in St. Louis to visit her elderly aunt.

I had intentions of continuing graduate studies based on my graduate study in Chinese history at Columbia and later at the School of Oriental and African Studies in London, and Berkeley seemed to be an appropriate place to do it. We saddled up Bublee and drove directly to Berkeley.

I have little recollection of our arrival at Berkeley, home of the Golden Bears. Several weeks later, we were ensconced in a boardinghouse with quite thin walls where a young couple very loudly made love in their bedroom next to ours. Irene was not pleased with the reception she received from the Modern India Project, being pooled with a collection of graduate students who knew only what they had read for classes. This was soon to change.

So, Irene had a job and I, with her support, decided to enroll in the graduate program in political science, particularly in the area of public policy. Originally, I had taken courses that focused on China, but found that what was offered was of poor quality. Having served overseas in the military and the CIA, I was allowed to enroll as a resident, and residents paid almost no tuition.

Since we had spent time in Asia, I did want to write a dissertation on Asia, particularly in the area of public policy. It was suggested that maybe I should take an interest in other parts of East Asia or Southeast Asia and look at Chinese communities there. Eventually, it was decided that it would be Indonesia. Irene and I worked out a proposal to go to Indonesia to do our research. We got a joint grant from the Ford Foundation. The original proposal was to go to China, but this was in 1956 and it was impossible for me to get into China to do any research. She did her research on the first Indian elections. We went through the whole idea of arranging to get out to Asia. She would go back and do her work on the Indonesian elections and I would work on the process of transferring domestic administration from the Dutch colonial period to independent Indonesia. I was to study the Chinese populations. By this time, I was interested in the Chinese community in Malaya and Indonesia, but they didn't speak the kind of Chinese that I knew and that has become the national language of China under the communist rule. So we enrolled in a class and started studying Indonesian, not Dutch. We were being taught in Arabic writing. We felt so smart because we could begin to write backwards. But, of course, they had already stopped using Arabic both in Malaya and in Indonesia. The thing that was interesting is that in Malaya they converted to British spellings and in Indonesia they started using Dutch spellings. So "Ship" would have been "Chip" in Singapore and "Tjip" in Jakarta.

We hardly ever did our homework. The teacher would tell us the etymology of almost every word in Indonesian. It showed to us that the background came from Dutch, from Arabic, from Portuguese, from all these different languages. It was fascinating. The thing I remember more than anything is that I could write in Arabic and I understood how they didn't write short vowels. Our daughter knows Arabic but she studied classical Arabic. When she went to Cairo no one could understand her because they were speaking colloquial Egyptian. She says that even today, some of the students that come from Saudi Arabia to study at PSU don't understand classical Arabic. So languages are very funny things.

After a while we were looking to improve our housing situation. My mother came to see us knowing that in our first seven years or so we had moved twelve times! She decided the only way we were going to settle down was if she offered us $15,000 to buy a house (in those days that was a fair amount of money). So then we went looking for a house. There was a young builder who was building a house in this area above Tilden Park on Wild Canyon Road. He thought we might be interested in it. He showed it to us and we were very interested in it. It was just the kind of house that we wanted to live in: a kind of modern wooden house. He agreed to sell it to us but, in the meantime, the real estate agent sold it to another person. However, he was willing to start another bigger house nearby, so he built this house and we spent a lot of time talking about what our preferences were. So we got a house built to our specifications.

The first house had been on level ground, but the second house was some distance away on a very steep hillside, so it meant that we would have to have a two-level house. The result was that there was more area shoved into two levels. You drove into the garage at the top level, the kitchen and combination living room/dining room were on the upper floor, and you had to go downstairs to the bedrooms. We loved that house and lived in it until we left for Indonesia.

CHAPTER SEVEN

Going to Indonesia

IRENE WAS PREGNANT AT THE TIME AND WANTING TO have the child in Indonesia because she knew that she would get a lot of domestic help if she gave birth to a child there. We took baby formula and a foldable baby carriage with us. My mother had been born and brought up in Japan and had not been back there since shortly before World War II, so the three of us took a Norwegian freighter from Los Angeles to Yokohama. (With all the luggage we couldn't take a plane.) We weren't sure what to do with our luggage, so the Norwegian captain suggested we leave it on his ship. We found out from the captain that the Norwegian and another Dutch boat would be in Norway and Singapore at just about the same time. They suggested we leave our stuff on the Norwegian boat and they would carry it to Singapore; we would take another boat from Osaka to Hong Kong, then on to Singapore. We spent a month in Japan visiting some places that were familiar to my mother and places that were familiar to me, in total spending about three weeks in Japan including a few days in Tokyo.

Also, Irene wanted to see pearl divers diving for pearls. We went to an island called Oshima, which was famous for its pearls, but there were no pearl divers around. So we came back to Atami on the main island, where we spent a day or so enjoying the hot baths and then west to Nagoya, including a side trip to Kagoshima where, we were told, there was active pearl diving going on. Other than that we did mostly touristy things. My mother was keen on walking. She wanted to go walking in all of the many gardens at every temple. Irene was pregnant and didn't feel like walking, so we had a little bit of a discussion about that. We took a side trip to Nara. Nara is the most beautiful city in Japan with lots of gardens and a classic medieval castle. Eventually we found our boat in Osaka. It was a fairly new freighter of Dutch registry and was still loading cargo.

It was supposed to be laden with concrete as part of reparations that Japan owed to Indonesia as a result of the Japanese role in World War II. However, there was continuous rain; worried the concrete would set, the captain decided that they were going to stop loading. They couldn't afford to stay longer in the port so the ship took off from Osaka, headed for Hong Kong, lightly loaded.

We were really enjoying the trip on the *Tjipanjet*. We were the only paying passengers, but there were other passengers on board. Apparently the company had a system where they allowed their officers to bring their families on various segments of the trips because they were so far away from Holland that they figured that they needed to be with their families once in a while. The captain had a wife along who was a very large woman. The mate had a wife and a young son.

On the way down to Hong Kong, the captain was informed that a typhoon was headed our way. He wanted to stay at sea and either ride out the typhoon there or go to

Hong Kong, but tying up in Hong Kong harbor was impossible because none of the ships in the Hong Kong harbor were going to leave. The company in Amsterdam thought the cost of riding out the storm at sea would be too expensive so they said we should go anchor in Junk Bay, a small bay just outside the harbor entry to Hong Kong. That was the worst place to ride out a typhoon. I remember there were anchors out in front and to the rear. The officers were instructing the crew as to when to release and when to let it float back. The wind wasn't constant and there were times when the wind would let up and the crew would pull and tighten the ropes.

At some point, after we must have spent six or seven hours doing this, a particularly strong gust hit the ship, the anchors pulled up out of the ground under the water, and the boat was blown against the rocks. I remember seeing the butter patties floating away as the sea flooded into the dining room. It was just six o'clock because the radio warned that the Kowloon ferry had been shut down. The engineer anticipating the crash had ordered all the cargo holds flooded. There we sat, tightly pressed against the cliff. The Chinese crew scrambled off the ship in the rain. The ship was at a sixty-degree angle! The hull was broken open and all the concrete that had been loaded kind of sealed the ship to the rocks. The angle meant that the lifeboat on that side of the ship was smashed while the lifeboat on the other side couldn't clear the hull. We sat on the corridor leading to the ship's bridge because it was narrow enough for us to brace ourselves against the wall opposite to the wall we were sitting against; also there was a stream flowing along the corridor where the rain blew into the ventilator.

At first light, the Hong Kong harbor police came to get us off: they rigged a rope ladder between the shore and the deck of the ship. Neither Irene nor I had very much trouble. We thought it was going to be really steep but, because the boat was at an angle, the shore wasn't that steep. They rigged it and put ropes on either side so you could walk across. They helped my mother, who was in her sixties, and the three of us got on the shore pretty quickly. The rotund wife of the captain had a good deal of trouble.

We were taken in hand by the Hong Kong police and escorted into town. All of a sudden we became, what would you say, objects of considerable interest to the population there. We were put up in the government guest house, which was very nice accommodations. Many Hong Kong residents were graduates of St. John's University in Shanghai and recognized our names from when my father went to teach there in 1904. He kept that job for forty years. My mother had been, among other things, the leader of the university choir. At this university, all of the classes had been in English. There was considerable demand among young Chinese of the upper classes because they always thought that they would probably go on and do graduate work overseas either in Europe or the United States. So there was a large English-speaking population in Shanghai; when we got to Hong Kong, all these people came out of the woodwork. They may not have known me or Irene but they certainly knew my mother and we were feted at all the best restaurants in Hong Kong.

There was a passenger ship owned by the same Dutch company. They figured that since we hadn't claimed any sort of compensation for experiencing a crash, they would treat us very well. They put us in the matrimonial suite in this passenger ship and we had very luxurious accommodations with all of our meals and cocktails on demand. They were quite happy to sponsor a reception in our name on the ship, ferrying all our hosts out to the ship. So we had a delightful stay in Hong Kong.

They were happy to accommodate us until the next ship

came in. There were two sister ships: one went from Japan to Singapore and one from Singapore to Surabaya. One was *Tjiluwah* and the other was *Tjiwangi*. The ship that crashed into the rocks was the *Tjipanjet*. The Dutch spell "chi" as in "cheese" with "tj." In Dutch the "J" sound is done with "dj". We named our son Tjip after that trip.

We took the *Tjiwanhi*, a second luxury passenger ship, down to Singapore, where our reception by the St. John's alumni was repeated. Happily the Norwegian ship, loaded with the baby stuff and all our extra luggage, was also in port and easily transferred to our ship for Surabaya.

We spent a couple of weeks in Malaya before going to Indonesia. They were looking forward to elections and Irene was in some demand as somebody who could give them an idea of what elections looked like. We spent a month in Singapore, where we bought a car, and drove up to Kuala Lumpur with my mother. We stopped and talked to various people along the way. English was pretty much understood by government servants. I also found out that in Malaya you could get along fine in English.

By this time, I was interested in the Chinese community, which was very large. I did find out that almost nobody in the Chinese community in Singapore, Malaysia, and later, in Indonesia, spoke the kind of Chinese that I spoke. I spoke what was the northern dialect and they had all come from the south and the southwest of China and spoke what is known as the Cantonese language and a few of the other sort of backwater languages. But they didn't use those really, and I didn't understand them.

CHAPTER EIGHT

Living in Indonesia

*W*HEN WE GOT TO INDONESIA, THOUGH, I FOUND that you couldn't use English, you had to use Dutch. I didn't know any Dutch, so the thing that we both had to do was to learn the Indonesian language, a very easy language. After having been through Chinese and Japanese, I found it a cinch. Since I mastered Japanese, it was particularly easy to learn Indonesian because both languages are monosyllabic. So, within a few months I was able to get along in Indonesian and the same was true with Irene.

While we were studying Indonesian, a young female lawyer, Soenarjati Hartono, who was also pregnant, helped Irene find a doctor and a hospital. When the baby arrived, the Dutch doctor was just about to be evacuated. The Dutch had agreed to give up Indonesia to the Indonesians except for the Dutch half of the island of New Guinea. Primarily, they realized that there were lots of natural resources that could be exploited there. A vote was taken in the United Nations as to whether this part of the island should go to Indonesia or Holland. Australia administered the other half of the island. The United Nations majority vote was to give it to Indonesia, and the Dutch were furious.

The Indonesians used this as a motive for removing anyone with Dutch citizenship from the country. Unlike the British, they had not educated locals to run any of the infrastructure apparatus such as the inter-island boats, the railroads, the post office, and the air transport system. They decreed that that they would not pay anybody who was usually paid by the Dutch. Specifically, they would not pay them in Indonesia, so the evacuees had to go to Holland to get their wages. The government sent out a lot of cruise ships to take all these evacuees back to Holland. In fact, since our doctor was paid by the government, three weeks after our son was born, the doctor went "home" to a country he had never seen.

In Surabaya we were put up in an old colonial hotel with yellow mosquito nets. It was not a place to bring a baby to so we sought a place to stay. We advertised in an English-speaking newspaper and received all sorts of ridiculous answers like pay a year's tuition for my son in California. But a tobacco exporter, Verloop, said maybe we could stay at his house for six months because he was planning on going home to see his wife and he knew that if he left his house vacant, Chinese people would move in. Verloop knew that if we moved in, we would leave.

We moved our things into his house before we had to return to Jakarta for orientation for three weeks. In Jakarta we lived in a Ford Foundation house and were driven everywhere, treatment more like a foreign service assignment than for students. We met various people and were told about not selling our dollars on the black market, which was half as expensive as the official market. Of course everybody in the Ford Foundation bought on the black market but it took us awhile to figure it out and we lost a fair amount of money by being good. As soon as we found out, we stopped doing that.

Verloop sent his driver to pick us up at the train station, and told us that tensions were so great he decided not to go back to Holland. Still he agreed to let us live in his house as promised. After six months his assistant moved in with him because he thought if there were two families in there—or two men at least—they would be able to hold the house because the anti-Dutch feeling was growing. Instead, we were offered the assistant's house, which was much more modest and in the flat part of Surabaya. Moreover, it happened to be on a road that was called Tjiptomangkusumo, which was named after a mythical Javanese hero. This road reinforced our naming our son Tjip. We lived there for six months, glad to have an air-conditioned bedroom, which was kind of unique.

This period in Surabaya gave us time to interview people in the city and to continue our study of the language. Irene had specialized in Indian elections, so she wanted to study the Indonesian elections and the elected assemblies. Having discarded the idea of studying the Chinese communities, I switched to a study of public policy. The thing was that Indonesia had just become independent at the time and they really did not have very much in the way of resources in the public policy field. Well, it so happened that USAID had agreed to provide a professor of public policy at an Indonesian training program in a place called Malang, in the hills above Surabaya; AID had offered the job to a professor working in Yogyakarta, but his wife did not want to move.

So the position was offered to me; a bonus was that it came with a small house. Malang was a very attractive town at 5,000 feet elevation as opposed to sea level. That makes a lot of difference. No one in the town spoke English, so we mastered the Indonesian language quickly and I was able to teach the students in this training program in Indonesian. Teaching at this institution gave me access to the public administrative establishment, both at the local and the national level. That was what I was observing and writing down for my dissertation.

I thought that if the administrators were into public policy, they needed to know something about what was going on in their jurisdictions, so I sent them out to various locations around Malang to do research on any kind of issues that were important in those areas. That was essentially the main thing that they did. I supervised this and talked to them about why it was important for them to know what was going on in their various assigned jurisdictions. So that was the nature of my involvement there. Because I was teaching at this academy, I had access to many officials in the administration of the Indonesian government. I remember I got to know the governor of East Java and the mayor of Malang and various county officials and so forth.

CHAPTER NINE

Return to the United States

a FTER TWO YEARS IN INDONESIA, OUR FINANCIAL SUP-
port from the Ford Foundation ended. We went back
to Berkeley and I eventually submitted my dissertation and
earned a PhD. While I was finishing my PhD, I went to the
Library of Congress in Washington to look at their Sino-
logical section, seeking sources on Indonesia. There, I met
a faculty member from American University. A new school
of International Service had been recently established. They
were just setting up a region-wide program of area studies
and they needed somebody in Southeast Asia. He set me up
to talk to the dean of this new program and I was offered a
job right then and there. I really didn't have all that much
choice because by this time I was forty years old, which is
a bit advanced to get into a collegiate program. But I was
lucky. I spent the next twenty-nine years in Washington

teaching at the School of International Service, which was focused exclusively on international affairs.

During that time, I was able to get back to Indonesia on numerous occasions. I also got to visit other countries in southeast Asia but especially Thailand and Malaysia. I wrote a number of papers and articles and I was used as a consultant by the State Department on numerous occasions on issues of Southeast Asia.

American University's School of International Service had been in existence only two years, but the dean was trying to flesh it out with specialists from all of the various regions of the world. With my Indonesian background, I guess I qualified, and they gave me the job of running the area studies program, which meant I taught mainly students who were involved or about be involved in Southeast Asia. This would have been in 1960/1961, and the U.S. government was becoming concerned about what was going on in Southeast Asia. So many of the people who showed up at my seminars, at my classes, were military, diplomatic, and other types of government officials. They wanted to learn more about Southeast Asia, so I was able to instruct them about goings-on in Southeast Asia. I had never been in Vietnam, but I had read a good deal and there wasn't all that much information available on Vietnam, so what little I knew was important. Of course I knew something about Malaysia and a lot about Indonesia.

I got my degree in 1962. Someone who was working for Irene agreed to type up the manuscript for my dissertation. I submitted the dissertation and then I had to go back to Berkeley for an oral examination. I also had to pass two language exams. One, fortunately, was in Indonesian, and I had no problem at all. The other one was French, which I hadn't used for a while. I was given a piece to translate; it was an article out of a magazine or something. I did it, but I know that the person on my orals committee said the translation was a bit "free"—but they accepted it anyway. So I was confirmed as a PhD. Then I flew back to Washington.

Initially, I had been given a faculty appointment at the School of International Service at American University. There was another school called the School of Public Administration. International Service was the international side of political science and Public Administration was mainly on the American side. It was decided between the two deans of the schools that, since I was a qualified political scientist, I should have a joint appointment. So my appointment was split but, frankly, as I look back on it, most of my efforts were in the international school. I remember that almost all of the graduate students on whose committees I served as a chairman were from international service, not from public administration. I did teach a course in the School of Public Administration on comparative government. That is to say: to compare American government with governments overseas. I taught variations on that course but never more than one course per semester. If I had an obligation to teach three courses, two were in international service and one was in public administration. That is pretty much how it went. As I say, I always identified myself as an international service faculty member.

American University had been established as a Methodist-affiliated university. There were all kinds of four-year colleges like Nebraska Wesleyan and other state institutions that were identified as Wesleyan or Methodist—Southern Methodist is one of the principal ones—but American University never worked out that way. It was created in the 1890s and almost immediately filled up with undergraduate students, so it just progressed as a normal university. During my stay there, I would say that the total student population was only about 13,000–15,000 students, pretty small for most universities. It's much larger now but, in those days, it was pretty small. And what's more, it had to compete with two other universities: Georgetown University and George Washington University. In international affairs, the Georgetown School of Foreign Service was internationally recognized as the school for men seeking careers in the foreign service of the State Department. The school at American University was designed to train people who work in international affairs in the public sector, that is to say, nongovernmental organizations. The School of International Service was created in 1957. I got there in 1960, so it was in its very early stages.

A very few years later, The Johns Hopkins University set up a School of Advanced International Studies or SAIS. It began to recruit a set of very well known faculty. Eventually, George Washington University set up its own school of International Affairs called the Elliott School of Foreign Affairs. There were four local institutes all competing for the same type of applicants: young people who were interested in foreign affairs. The American University School of International Service had to compete with all of these other institutions, most of which were better known than American University.

As a Methodist institution, the university had chosen its president, ever since its founding, from candidates who were a minister or bishop of the Methodist church. Not long after I joined the faculty, Hurst Robins Anderson had served as the president for maybe fifteen years and wanted to retire. A presidential search committee was formed. At that time, I was the secretary of the faculty association at American University, and so the chair and I were selected to represent the faculty on the presidential recruitment committee. We looked at a number of people, both part of the Methodist establishment and others. The person that we eventually decided upon, with the strong support of the faculty representatives, was George H. Williams, who had been the vice-president of New York University. We got him passed and he turned out to be a Catholic, which some people thought would dry up funds from a lot of people who gave money to the university as a Methodist institution. Williams didn't last all that long though, as he got other offers after he had served for five years.

During Williams's tenure, he asked me to serve as an assistant provost to work out of the president's office. On occasion, I was sort of handling the relationship between this new president and the faculty of the university. There was some resistance on the part of the faculty, and I was supposed to deal with this resistance. There was also a dean of the School of International Service whose function was to go out and get financial support from alumni and so forth. Therefore, he needed to get somebody to run the school and, because I was the associate dean, I handled the internal matters within the school while the dean was constantly going outside to raise money. I did this for three or four years. While I had this position, there was an uprising. I think it was an anti–Vietnam war demonstration and I was supposed to deal with it. Mostly students were protesting any involvement in the Vietnam war. I remember I was working out of the president's office, which was an old house. The students came and held a sit-in like they did everywhere else.

I had completed a profile of a province in Thailand on the border of Vietnam. The Chao Phraya River flowed in-between but it looked as though maybe this would be a good basis for the establishment of an American military base to strike at Vietnam. It never happened and I didn't realize at the time that I was essentially doing this for the defense department. So I did have that kind of contact with the war in Vietnam. What's more, I was giving courses on Southeast Asia, and many of the students in those courses were members of the armed services. So, I guess if anyone was to blame for the protest, it was me rather than any of the other faculty or administration. The students occupied the president's office and they routed me out of my office. Even though I contributed to the American efforts in Vietnam, I was opposed to the war and I went to demonstrations protesting the war.

I essentially didn't like being assistant to the president so I argued myself out of that position and back into teaching. I taught courses about Vietnam until 1965. Between 1960 and 1965, we had two more children, both daughters: Janet and Joro. We lived on Drummond Avenue in West Chevy Chase. What you had there in West Chevy Chase was a community called Somerset that had a city charter. Somerset had a number of facilities such as tennis courts and a swimming pool. Just up the street and across Wisconsin Avenue was the Norwood Parish School; Tjip and Janet went to their preschool. Joro went to a preschool that was on the way to AU so I could drive her. My mother, Ahma, decided that we ought to baptize the kids, so we chose the Norwood church. Aunt Jerry was their honorary godmother; she flew from California to be there. I remember that on the day of the baptism, Tjip wasn't feeling well and later he came down with mumps. We have pictures of him looking miserable.

MIL AND IRENE IN THEIR WEDDING DRESS IN THE GARDEN
BEHIND THEIR APARTMENT ON RATENDON ROAD, NEW DELHI

CROSSING THE INDIA OCEAN ON THE S.S. KARANJA

MIL AND THE GUARD WATCHING ELEPHANTS AT MADANDA ROCK

MIL AND BUBLEE NEAR LAKE VICTORIA

AS THE ELEVATION INCREASED SLIGHTLY,
BUBLEE BECAME STUCK IN THE SAND

WALL PAINTING SHOWING REVOLUTIONS BY YEAR AT THE ENTRANCE
TO A GOVERNMENT BUILDING IN BANGKOK. MIL STANDS IN FRONT.

TJIPANDJET - OUR BOAT FROM OSAKA TO HONG KONG
SUNK AT THE ENTRANCE OF HONG KONG HARBOR

MIL HOLDING AN UNHAPPY TJIP BEING ROWED TO SHORE WHILE
OUR BOAT TAKES ON IN COCONUTS IN THE PHILIPPINES

BALI DANCERS AT ART VILLAGE IN CENTER OF THE ISLAND

MIL BEFORE JAPANESE HOTEL IN TOKYO
DESIGNED BY FRANK LLOYD WRIGHT

MALANG, INDONESIA, TJIP IN HIS BAMBOO PUSHCART

TJIP, JANET IN BABY WALKER WITH IRENE IN
WALNUT CREEK, CA – AT THE LARIEU'S

SWIMMING ON THE SOUTH COAST OF JAVA IN COVE
PROTECTED FROM SHARKS AN HOUR SOUTH OF MALANG

MIL IN TRISHAW IN JOGJAKARTA AS WE
DRIVE FROM MALANG TO JAKARTA

MIL PLAYING IN SAME POOL

MIL SQUIRTING WATER ON TJIP ON DESK OF OUR
HOUSE IN WILDCAT CANYON ROAD, BERKELEY

MIL WITH TJIP AND BABY JANET IN THE BACKYARD
OF OUR CHEVY CHASE HOME

MIL AND CHILDREN ON THE FRONT STEPS OF OUR
CHEVY CHASE HOUSE ON DRUMMOND AVE.

CHAPTER TEN

Family Travel Abroad

THEN, IN 1965, WE TOOK THE KIDS TO INDIA! WE HAD two different fellowships: Irene was going to go to India and I was going to go to Southeast Asia. We took my mother and three children with us to India. First, we stopped with Ahma and the kids in Switzerland to go skiing. The town nearby was called Wildhaus. We went skiing both in Switzerland and Austria. The ski slopes were gentle, very good for kids. We were there over Christmas and we had a Christmas tree and I remember we had brought a set of Legos for the kids and we spent a lot of time playing with them. We were put up in rooms all together. The kids were all in one room and we were paying for room and board. Joro, the youngest one, was only about two and they decided to charge her not half price but full price! When we left, Irene refused to pay full price and had a big fight with the hotel. When we got to the airport, they wouldn't let us into the boarding area because they said we hadn't paid the bill. Irene told them the circumstances and showed them little Joro. They just laughed and let us through.

We flew to Karachi because Irene's father was Science Attaché there. Irene's parents were renting a summer house on the beach and we all went there. They had a guy playing a flute with a cobra and the kids were all around watching. We went along the shore and the kids rode on one-humped camels on the beach. Irene's father and stepmother, and my mother, were there. Back in Karachi, Irene did some interviewing because we were on a study trip. Then we went up to Peshawar and again Irene was doing some study. First we had gone to Rawalpindi, which is where they were moving the embassy to. So some of the people she was interviewing were up in Karachi and some were in Rawalpindi. The people we were staying with were in USAID. Irene wanted to go out to a village and interview people and they arranged that. She was studying how the Pakistanis were introducing democracy—or what they were calling basic democracy (it wasn't very democratic).

So Irene went out to the villages to interview, and both little girls started wandering around and crawling around on the floor, which is not a good idea out in the bush like that. I guess they got stuff on their hands or licked their fingers because later, when we got to New Delhi, they were both sick. It turned out they both had worms. But they had different kinds! They are easy to cure if you get to them soon enough. We flew to New Delhi and we stayed in a guest house provided by the organization we got the grant from, and they had a rooftop because the houses were close together. If you wanted to get cool you could go up on the roof. Janet had a doll made out of a sock that she carried all over. She wasn't that old, so she would chew on it. A monkey came and took it away from her and she was devastated. I remember writing to a friend, asking him to send him out one like the first, but of course by the time it came she had forgotten about it.

When we were staying in the guest house, we arranged for Joro and Janet to go to a little playschool around the corner. We didn't stay in that Ford guest house for more than three weeks. We moved to the Maidens Hotel, which had a swimming pool, and we had a suite with three or four bedrooms. We had room and board there and they had good Indian style: they always brought us tea and biscuits in the morning. Both Janet and Tjip went to the school. All together we stayed there about a year. At one point in our travels we were in Orissa (now known as Odisha), where there was a procession with a cart holding gods, and people threw flowers under it and they threw themselves under it.

I went on to Southeast Asia, where I had a couple of special assignments. One was in Thailand to do a profile of a province on the Thai border of Vietnam to essentially determine the answers to "What was the culture?" and "What was the attitude towards the central government?" and so forth. The name of the province was Sakon Nakhon. I spent three months in Thailand doing this research and then I moved down to Malaysia.

When I was in Thailand, I talked to the governor and some people in the governor's office and the Thai military commander there. These were the only people who could speak any English, and I didn't know any Thai. They gave me some statistics, and there was some problem in the province about groups in the province who spoke different languages. Some of them spoke Thai, some of them spoke Lao, and some of them spoke Vietnamese.

The war in Vietnam had started when Ho Chi Minh and the Viet Cong defeated the French in North Vietnam and began to move south. Then they ran up against the British and kind of got stuck there. The British did not want to remain in Vietnam so, essentially, their role was taken up by the Americans, who got more and more involved. There wasn't actually any major fighting at that time, 1965 and 1966; the war hadn't really accelerated.

I was doing work in Malaysia and Irene was still in India. She went down to Sri Lanka and then to Madras and to Kuala Lumpur. I had a grant called the Southeast Asia Development Advisory Group, SEA-DAG, from an outfit called Philco TechRep. That grant was what I used in Malaysia (formerly Malaya; this change occurred during the mid-1960s).

A friend of mine had already been in Malaysia and he suggested that I work with the government of Malaysia on what they called a community development program. The issue there was that much of Malaysia had been taken over by the British, who cleared the jungle and put in rubber trees. They employed a lot of the Indian population. When Malaysia was turned over by the British to the Malaysians, the new government of Malaysia wanted to do something for the indigenous population because they felt that this group, who were being left out of everything else, would be a good subject for communist penetration. I was asked to do an evaluation of the many plantations that were turned into settlements for the indigenous population. Because there is very little difference between the Indonesian language and the Malaysian language, I could get along in Malay.

So I did an evaluation of these settlements. I talked to various people, I went to various locations, often with the help of some Peace Corps volunteers, to come in contact with people who were either living in or running these community development settlements. They consisted of a number of houses that were built by the government and occupied by the indigenous population. The settlements were set up as a community of houses, all of them identical, with what they call a "kitchen garden," a garden where a family can raise fruits and vegetables or keep livestock. The men were supposed to go out and work on rubber estates. I found that the residents of these settlements were very unhappy because they didn't like working on the rubber plantations. One of the things that didn't appeal to the Malay workers was that they had to show up at four o'clock in the morning to start tapping the rubber trees. Most of the residents that I spoke to were quite unhappy with the situation, and they wanted to do a lot of other different things like set up small grocery stores, travel services, or purchase vehicles to take people into town. Most of the Malaysian men had never worked on an estate before because those positions had always been occupied by Indians.

However, the government of Malaysia insisted that all of these communities stick to the original plan. Another complication, and a slightly later development, was that they set up even more of these communities but, instead of producing rubber, they produced palm oil from palm trees. Rubber trees take four years to really mature but palm trees mature in six months to a year. So the people in these newer programs were actually getting rewards for their activities long before the others, and they had enough money to go into town and enjoy. This made the original settlers increasingly annoyed with the whole situation. There wasn't very much that I could do about it except submit a report that was critical of what the Malaysian government had decided on. I went out to various communities in a variety of provinces.

I came back to Kuala Lumpur when Irene flew in from Sri Lanka, and we had sort of a second honeymoon on Turtle Beach in Kuala Besut, which was in the state of Kuala Terengganu in Malaysia. We saw turtles, and they cried while they were releasing their eggs. We had planned to go to Indonesia, but were unable to get a visa because of the ongoing trouble there. The president, Sukarno, was being removed from office by the military. The military commander, Suharto, took over and there was mass killing by the military, which was anti-communist. So we went to Kuching, the principal city in Sarawak, Malaysia, and stayed in the American consulate, then from there to Sibu.

Irene remembers that she was so tired of gin and tonics and she was served the first Campari soda she ever had. That person was the one who helped arrange for us to go inland. We went up the Rajang River on a boat to Kapit. He arranged for us to go up this river to visit some of the longhouses because they were the last elements of real democracy in the area. The longhouses were built on stilts with a shared veranda for everybody, and the individual families had rooms behind them. Then we got transportation to the farthest river to the west.

That's where we attended a special ceremony. I had to drink rice liquor every time they told me to, and I got so drunk that I fell down the steps. You see, everything there is built on piles. Irene drank one and said, "I can't anymore, I am pregnant." I kept drinking. I was going along with them. You know, I was observing the custom. Another guy kept going outside and throwing up. Well, the thing is, I think they told the girl with the "chicken" to come to me more often than anybody else. I was out for three days. They took me back down the river and I was just out of everything. Irene was worried. She hoped the consul was going to come back for us.

After we got back to Kuching, we tried to go to Burma on a three-day pass and the plane was delayed and we never went because by the time we got there, we'd have to turn around and come right back. The thing is they only had one plane a week. They didn't really want visitors. It wasn't until later in 1970 that we went back in that area. So we went back to Delhi, and Ahma and the kids flew to Karachi.

Irene was on a government-funded scholarship, so they would pay for transportation of our household goods. We had bought several rugs and we were able to send them back. We took them all down to Bombay and put them on a boat, and then we took the boat to Karachi. It was an Italian passenger ship with two funnels. The funnels had some kind of flaring behind each funnel to keep the smoke from coming down on the passengers. In Karachi we picked up Ahma and the kids and then went on to Venice. That's where Joro got lost under the tables.

We were in the open area in front of the cathedral, The Doge or something like that. There were lots of tables where people could sit and drink. We were sitting there and all of a sudden Irene or I looked around and we were missing one child. We rushed around looking. It wasn't very far to the water. We were so worried that we reported a lost child to the police. We spent quite awhile searching the location for her, and there she was under the table picking up the bottle caps.

I made arrangements to pick up a new Fiat and drive to Genoa to catch another boat. We also hired a new au pair, Heidi, who stayed with us three years I think. She was the best au pair we ever had. We got on the ship and when we got to New York, the car was on a different ship. We hired a big Chrysler station wagon and about halfway between New York and Washington D.C., we had a flat tire. We were on the main highway and we had to pull over with three kids, and somebody stopped to help us change tires. After we got back to Washington, I went back to New York to pick up the Fiat and bring it to Washington.

I continued teaching and of course the possibility of war with Vietnam was even more critical. I was asked by the State Department to give a number of talks on what I knew about Vietnam and the surrounding countries. So I did quite a bit of that. Then, from 1965 to 1970, the Vietnam war was very much at its peak. So I was in demand as somebody who specialized in Southeast Asia.

CHAPTER ELEVEN

USAID

URING TWO YEARS AT USAID I WAS WORKING FOR
Jack Sullivan, a former student of mine. He had taken
a couple of my courses when I had first arrived to teach at
A.U. He wrote a doctoral dissertation about Indonesia, and I
was the chairman of his dissertation committee.

From 1979 to 1981 I was on leave from the University
and assigned to USAID. The State Department had an
arrangement with universities where they would accept a
person to work in the department from a university and they
would pay the university the salary so they could employ
somebody else to pick up the vacancy. One of the principal
things I did in USAID was to be a consultant to their Indonesian program. I went out to Indonesia in 1980 to assess
what they needed in order to have a decent administrative
service. I traveled from Jakarta to Yogyakarta to Surabaya
and over to Makassar, which at that time was called Ujumg
Padang, one of the southern cities of Southern Sulawesi, and
over to Pontianak in Kalimantan to see where five training
centers should be located. I went to Sumatra too. In 1980

I wrote a fairly substantial report identifying five locations for the local government training program to set up training centers. USAID appropriated $13 million for the Indonesian government to use in setting up these centers.

So I spent two years in the State Department focusing on Southeast Asia. After that, I came back and I did a couple of short-term consultancies with the State Department on administration policy. I went to a number of countries in Southeast Asia and South Asia. I spent some time in Nepal, Sri Lanka, and in what was known as Burma, and I got to be pretty familiar with the entire area.

During this time, Tjip and Mary Beth were married on August 28, 1982, in a very fancy wedding. The mother of the bride does the arrangements. They were all fixated on Irene's book about street foods, so for the reception they had little tables with different street foods on them. That wedding was a traditional church wedding except they had each person say one sentence or so during the ceremony.

In 1983 I joined a team that went to Pakistan. I was taken on as a South Asian specialist. There were about four of us. The leader of the group didn't know very much about South Asia so he depended on me. The AID mission in Pakistan was not at all active because Pakistan had resumed activity on their nuclear facility and therefore the United States had stopped its aid to Pakistan. But that didn't prevent us from going to Pakistan to make an assessment of what AID should be doing if Pakistan could be persuaded to stop its nuclear activity. I remember I was assigned to the northern part of Pakistan, and I went to Peshawar and the Center for Rural Development. Nothing much came from that. During our stay in Pakistan we were met by the president, whose name was Muhammad Zia-ul-Haq. In retrospect, I think that he was responsible for all the difficulties that Pakistan is facing today because he promoted the Islamic extremists.

He released many Mullahs who had been interned previously and arranged for them to be set back up with their congregations. With Muhammad Zia-ul-Haq, Pakistan lost its characteristic as a secular country as the Mullahs gained much more community influence than they had before.

In 1983, our daughter Janet took a year off from Radcliffe to spend the year in Cairo on a Fulbright. She stayed another year, and we had all these tickets on Pan Am that had to be used up. So we arranged for the two girls and us to go visit. We also went to Dubrovnik in Croatia, Corfu, Athens, and Delphi.

That's when Irene broke her arm on a motor bike in Samos. She and a truck tried to share a bridge and the truck won of course, and she was knocked off the bridge and broke her arm. They said that if she went back to them, they would give her free treatment but we wanted to go to Turkey in a boat up the coast to Ephesus where there were the Greek ruins and the salt plains, which were wonderful. And then we went to Istanbul for a couple of days and we made arrangements to go home one day early with Joro. We couldn't stay as long as planned because Irene had to get her arm looked after. Janet went back to Cairo.

Irene had to get her arm attached properly. They had said we had fourteen days before Irene's arm would start to attach incorrectly, so when we got to New York and called the doctor, Irene said, "Look, it has to be done within seven days and that's tomorrow." They stuck a piece of metal in it. After a year, Irene said, "My arm is doing fine and I can't stand the metal," so they took it out.

Incidentally, Pan Am's generosity with our tickets was the reason that they went under; they went bankrupt because there were too many people using them and nobody paying for the seats. So the last time we flew on Pan Am, a couple years later, it looked like nobody had upgraded the plane; I wondered if the company would fall apart. They went under pretty quickly, which is kind of too bad because they were a very good airline for a long time.

CHAPTER TWELVE

The Mid-1980s to 1990s

1985

IN 1985 WE WENT TO CAMEROON IN AFRICA, WHERE Tjip and Mary Beth were serving as Peace Corps volunteers. Irene took off in July for Africa. She stopped in Cameroon, but I was sick when she went over, so I followed her about a week or so later. I remember I was sitting in an airport in Cameroon and I was the only person in the airport! Irene, Tjip, and Mary Beth were supposed to pick me up there, but they couldn't find the airport!

The major city, the capital of Cameroon, is Yaoundé. Tjip and Mary Beth were in the highlands of English-speaking Cameroon, the part of Cameroon that is closest to Nigeria. Nigeria had been an English colony, so those nearest to Nigeria spoke English. We stayed for another two weeks or so in Cameroon, and then we went to Nairobi.

It was the Third World Conference on Women, and I

went with Irene to all the NGO meetings. I don't think I did much but stand on the sides and watch what was going on. All I remember is the fact that I was among the very few males at that conference. I went to some of the sessions and I remember people looked at me as though I was an imposter.

1987

Then for a few years I was teaching back in the United States and serving as the Associate Dean of the School of International Service at American University. The dean of the school became become too ill and I was named acting dean. We were looking for a replacement (I had no intention of becoming the dean because the dean's principal job is soliciting money and has very little to do with what goes on at the school). We were in the market for a replacement dean. We found a man named Gregory Wolfe, who had been the president of Portland State University. He had taken leave from the university to run for Congress on the Democratic ticket. He lost in the primary, he was at loose ends, and we hired him. This was not a good choice. He spent all of his time downtown at the Cosmos club. After about two years, he agreed to retire. He went down to Florida International University, where he secured a faculty position. We found an excellent replacement for him in Lou Goodman, who stayed on long after I left. I remember his specialty was Latin America. We went to a number of faculty receptions at his house.

Irene had a part-time appointment at American University to teach women's studies. In 1987, Irene got a Fulbright Fellowship and I got a faculty exchange appointment with the university in Sri Lanka. Irene's fellowship was supposed to be half time in Nepal and half in Sri Lanka. We went to Sri Lanka together, and all the universities were closed because of an assassination. We didn't have anything to do so we traveled around. We took a side trip to the Maldives. We talked to various NGOs and we went up to Peradeniya, where the intellectuals and researchers were. There was a woman from Sri Lanka, Vidyamali Samarasinghe, who was (and is) on the faculty at A.U.

In Nepal all the students were on strike. We got an SUV and they took us around to where they were teaching civil servants. Then we went to Lumle, where they taught English to the Nepali Gurkhas who were joining the army (really they were joining the guard for English establishments all over the world). Anyway, we had to go up the escarpment and we had a couple of sherpas accompany us because we couldn't carry our packs. So we spent three months in Nepal. Irene mostly concentrated on community forestry and wrote a very academic paper about it. Irene got a call when we were in Nepal about interviewing for a tenure track position in Berkeley. She went back and had one day to rest and then had to give a lecture. She gave one lecture to cover the three different departments that were interested: Politics, Environment, and Urban Studies. When we got back to Washington, she was offered the job. It took a year to go back and get things straightened out, and then we moved the next year.

1988

Before we moved to Berkeley, in 1988 we were trying to sell the house on Drummond Avenue in West Chevy Chase, and we got hit with a downburst that knocked down all the trees on the property. It's sort of like a tornado except for the fact that it's a downdraft instead of an updraft. It's like an upside-down tornado; instead of sucking things up, it blows them down. It went up our street so it didn't hit any houses, but across the street, on the major highway where the houses were in the other direction, it tore into the homes and it took a lot of the roofs off.

1989

Irene was offered a full professorship at UC Berkeley. I had decided I did not want to live a continent away from her so I retired from American University and I went with her to UC Berkeley. We bought a car to drive across the country. During that drive we went to Seattle to visit Irene's brother's family: Jack and Mary. No sooner had we arrived in Berkeley that we got news that Ahma, my mother, had died. She had cancer. She had been on the hospice side of the rest home where she had lived for a long time. She was already in the hospice when we left. So almost immediately we flew back to Washington and participated in what was not so much a funeral, because that had already been held, but a memorial service.

The year 1989 brought the Loma Prieta earthquake on October 17, where much of San Francisco shook and where the houses that were built on the fill in the downtown part of San Francisco all collapsed because there was no stability. The approaches to the Bay Bridge were destroyed. So, in order to get over to San Francisco, one had to go all the way down and around to a different bridge to get over. We didn't go over so much. The Richmond–San Rafael Bridge was a long way around because it went over to Marin County, not to San Francisco, and then from Marin County you had to get down to San Francisco. It was really a long trip, and most of our best friends lived in San Francisco rather than the East Bay. One recollection I have of that house is that it had a swimming pool and when the earthquake shook, the waves went back and forth in the pool.

We were renting that house. Irene was teaching and I

was at loose ends, so I worked with a real estate agent to see what kind of housing was available and what we would like. We found a house on the hill above the Claremont Hotel on Canyon View Lane in Oakland. It was a fairly steep hill. There were 164 steps. When we got up there, it was just what we wanted and we learned that you could gun up your car and go up the hill and, if you were careful, you could turn around without going over the hill. You could get in trouble. If you kept going straight, you would go over the hill. One woman made a turn at the top of the hill and almost drove right into our house.

It was a lovely house, with a paved flat area where we could leave our car. It had a beautiful view of San Francisco Bay. It was a typical California house of all wood and glass with these tremendous glass windows that opened up towards the bay. It had to be tied down before we could buy it. There was no basement so they drove some piles down, I think, and screwed it in so it wouldn't fall off the hill. And everything inside the house was also screwed down. It had been there for five years or so. It had three bedrooms and two bathrooms, a sitting area, and a big sort of study area. It was on this sort of canyon and you could see the fog coming in on either side but it didn't hit us: these microclimates!

1990

In 1990 our first grandchild, Tjip and Mary Beth's son Eliot, was born, which was the same year Janet was married in Chicago. There was an HIV problem in Cameroon. Anyone who was in the establishment was brought home to have give birth in the States. So when Mary Beth got pregnant, she was brought home and went to her family's house in Greencastle, Indiana, and that's where she had Eliot. Tjip arranged, as he could, to get there for the birth. Mary Beth was there for about two or three months, and the grandmother took care of the baby while Mary Beth went to Chicago to participate in Janet's wedding. So we went up there, and Janet and John were married in a chapel on the Chicago campus. We were very pleased with the man she had chosen for her husband. We hadn't liked the previous boyfriend at all.

The chapel was on campus, and John's sister's husband was a minister, so he did the honors. There was a baby and I remember the baby's mother had to walk out with it because the baby was crying. They had the reception at the student house and it was a lunch. It wasn't a big deal. We gave all of the kids $300 or something like that and let them do what they wanted. So that covered their dresses and everything.

In 1990 we took a trip to Taiwan, Indonesia, and Papua New Guinea. We went to Indonesia twice during 1990. The second time we also went to Bangladesh and Nepal, and it had to do with housing. That December, when we flew out, we missed Christmas and when we got to Indonesia there were more Santa Clauses than there were anywhere even though it's a Muslim country. The same thing was true when we got to Thailand. They seem to have adopted all this ridiculous stuff. There was a conference about urban development and Irene went as a representative of Berkeley to Indonesia. We stopped in Taiwan and she gave some talks.

While in Papua New Guinea we took a trip up the river and we spent a few days in Port Moresby. That was when we expected to be met by a Fulbright student who had been at American University. The family had a wedding but all of the wedding presents were stolen! We went out in December and didn't come back until January 1991 when Bush declared war on Iraq. I went home directly across the Pacific, and Irene was going west to give a report to Geneva or somewhere about what we had studied, and they had redirected all of the airplanes to go around and they also confiscated all of the computers because they were afraid that some of them might be geared to blow up. She didn't think she would see her computer ever again but, actually, they mailed it to us as soon as she got home. I didn't have that trouble.

1991-1992

In 1991, we had recently moved into this lovely house when there was a big fire in October that began in Oakland. It had been started by a cigarette that someone had thrown out. The fire people had gone and put it out. However, these were urban fireman, who didn't know that you had to dig down and be sure that there weren't roots that were still hot. What happened? The wind came up the next day and, before anybody knew it, the whole hill was on fire. We were at a restaurant looking out across to San Francisco and all of a sudden we could see that the shades were starting to go up because it was getting quite dark. Before that, it had been very bright, but the smoke had darkened the sky. Also, the top of the waves looked quite greasy. So we said, "Where is this all coming from?" We turned around and you could see that the hills were on fire. Our son was watching the baseball game and they actually stopped the ball game for a while and told everybody what was happening, which is very unusual. He was really worried but by that time he couldn't call. We went back up the hill to our house and there were policeman at the bottom saying, "You can't go up there." We said, "Well, our house is up there," and he said, "You have twenty minutes to get what you want." So I remember the people who we were driving with took everything out of the front closet, which was our old coats and stuff, which wasn't very important. Irene got the computer and her students' papers and some clothes in laundry baskets. She didn't think about shoes and was actually wearing flip-flops. But we got out of there pretty fast.

Then I snuck out back because there was a road that went to houses above ours that apparently wasn't being monitored by law enforcement. I went up that road and sort of slid down the hill to our place and I got the hose to water the roof of the house until I realized that I wasn't doing any good at all. And, at that point, it seemed to me that the fire was moving farther and farther away from where our house was. And what's more is that on Claremont Avenue, which was a gorge, the fire personnel took up stations along this street and could have been very fortunate because, just below the entrance to our driveway, there was a reservoir at the bottom of the hill and the fire trucks could fill up and spray the falling ashes as they returned up the hill to the fire. This should have been useful except for the fact that the visiting fire department didn't have the right kind of screws to fit into the hydrant, so it was useless. The fire hydrants in Berkeley and Oakland were different sizes because of the way that the municipal boundaries were drawn. The boundaries had been drawn to keep students from coming and having drinks at the Claremont Hotel, so the lines weren't straight, and it was very confusing. City and regional planning did a study afterwards and one of the things they suggested is that they should all have the same size screws on the hydrants. And the other thing is that there should be a fire station up at the top during fire season. So they built one that would also be a community meeting place the rest of the year. This way, they had somebody who could look down as well as look up. The fire was devastating, with 2,500 houses or apartments burned. Something like twenty-five people were killed because they were all trying to drive down these roads and got all backed up. So some people tried to jump into swimming pools. But the swimming pools were boiling.

Not only did their houses burn, but so did the cars that they were using to escape from the fire. After we were evacuated, we were watching and listening to the fire just below the Claremont Hotel and you could hear the cars popping as they blew up. It was scary. But the wind pushed the fire across the freeway and it went into Oakland instead of coming down into Berkeley. So we were saved. When we got back into the house there were all these calls on our telephone asking if we were okay, but of course we hadn't been there to answer. Because it was assumed that almost everyone in that area had lost everything, we kept getting insurance claims to see if we had lost anything. A lot of the faculty lost their houses. One of the women had taken out all her notes but, when the fire came, she walked out and left them because she got all excited. The next day they didn't have classes. The day after that, Irene went into her lecture with her flip flops on and nobody cared. But if the flames had come to our house, they would have gone right over the hill and down to the Berkeley campus. It was that close. It was pretty scary. A fire is worse than an earthquake because there is nothing left. After that, we pulled out all the Scotch broom as well as the eucalyptus because they burn very fast. We put in different kinds of plants in the hill behind us, so the fire changed our vegetation to some extent.

From December 1991 to January 1992, we went down to visit our friend Ruth, who had a farm in Costa Rica. We stayed in the house next door. We went on to one of the coasts. We rented a car and drove down to the port across the sound from the island and took a boat out to one of the islands and we snorkeled. We also saw a variety of pretty birds.

Then, in the summer, we went to China by way of Hong Kong. In those days, it was very difficult to get into China. We were taken into China by Irene's friend who was teaching in Guangzhou. In those days, China was not welcoming to foreigners. From there, we went to Bangkok, and met a friend who helped us go into Laos because he was representing the Asia Development bank there. These were areas that were not easy to get to. Then we flew from there to Hanoi. Irene was trying to collect information about what was happening in Southeast Asia for her courses. Hanoi was still very much a French town, very charming. We went to see the prison where John McCain had been held. The compulsory thing was going to see his prison. We had lovely dinners because they were still serving very French meals. We had some currency and you couldn't take it out; it was worth nothing. So we spent it on nice dinners and then we flew home.

Joro was married two years after Janet, in August 1992. She is sort of a contrarian: she decided she wanted a black dress, not a white one. She wanted to get married up in the hills above Salt Lake City. Her husband was a "Jack Mormon," so there weren't going to be many Mormons there because if you are a "Jack Mormon," you get kicked out of the church and nobody wants to have anything to do with you. So, except for his family and one uncle from California, there were no people from his side. Since we had to fly in, there weren't too many people from ours either. Irene's brother and his wife came from Seattle, of course Dorothy was there, and that was about it. We went up to Sun Valley where they have a resort. We rented a big house with lots of rooms with hot tubs. The kids went hiking and we watched the kids. So that was very nice.

Then, shortly after that, Irene was invited to go to a conference in Esalen about women leaders. In the summer they have massages out in the sun and people with no clothes on. The conference was kind of dull, but halfway through, her cousin, who was very important in her life, died. So she used that as a reason to get out of the rest of this conference and flew to Wilmington. The next year, Joro graduated from law school. She had never told us how well she did. She graduated at the top of the class, and was sort of the valedictorian.

Irene had a very distinguished career. She was assigned to Urban and Regional Planning and Women's Studies. She was eventually appointed the first chair of the first department of Women's Studies anywhere in the University of California system. I was used as what was known as an adjunct lecturer, which is the lowest academic position. The thing is, I wasn't worried about status. I didn't have to go to faculty meetings, which is nice, and what's more, I could sort of pick and choose the courses that I wanted to teach.

So the next nine years, we were in Berkeley and almost every semester I taught one course, many of which were in the department of city and regional planning. Since public affairs, particularly at the local level, had been my specialty, I taught courses on comparative urban government in a variety of countries. On one occasion, I had a course that took me into the central valley of California, to central towns down there to see how they were handling their public affairs. What I was focusing on is the effect of economic change on public policy. And those towns in the central valley were undergoing change primarily because the railroad system in that part of California was almost going out of existence. There were populations, particularly in areas such as melon production, that were dependent upon the railroads getting their product to the urban areas. These people, mostly African Americans, were left without a consumer for their products, so what I was trying to do was talk with them about what they could do as an alternative to farming melons.

My courses in the valley involved each of the students taking a different city and deciding what they should do and presenting alternatives. Students went out and studied and then they came and the class talked about it together. It was a really interesting community activity. It was called

The Micropolitics of Development. I taught that both at the undergraduate level and the beginning graduate level. Well, actually, I didn't create it; it was created by someone else, but he was appointed full professor at the University of California at Davis. He departed and I was left with the whole graduate program in Urban and Regional Planning. Graduate students would go out and talk to various people, mostly what you might call decision makers in various towns, and come back and report in class in front of all the other students, so that there was a constant exchange.

1993

The next time I was asked by USAID to help was in about 1993 while we were living in Berkeley. They asked me to create something called the Asia Democracy Program. I went to the Philippines, to Indonesia, Thailand, Bangladesh, Nepal, and Sri Lanka to see what AID missions were doing in terms of community development in those countries. I started out in the Philippines and I was in Manila for a few days, talking to people at the University in Quezon City. Then I went down to Cebu. One of the problems is that the provincial government is dominated by the big families in the Philippines. They are the ones who decide who is going to run the country. Frankly, I reported on this and said that there wasn't very much we could do about it as long as those well-to-do families ran the country.

Then I went on to Thailand. I had a number of contacts there, mainly at the university. The name of the principal university in Bangkok is Tribhuvan University. Tribhuvan is the Harvard of Thailand. There is another university, Thammasat University, which has more functional programs. There were courses that had to deal with democracy, local government, and public administration, which is what I was particularly interested in.

Then I went on to Nepal, where I encountered Julia Bloch, who was ambassador to Nepal. She had been appointed ambassador by President Nixon. Although I was there during the Carter administration, somehow she was there because her husband gave money to everybody. She kind of dismissed me because I had suggested that the program wasn't working. I found that she had her own agenda. She wasn't interested in what I was saying. She had no interest in what I was planning to look at in Nepal.

Then I moved on to Sri Lanka. Because of my university background, I kind of automatically chose to talk to university people about the condition of democracy. Usually, they were the best people to talk to. I did talk to several government people in Colombo, but they were part of a bureaucratic superstructure. They had no interest in promoting self-government and democracy because that took up their time; they would rather not be involved. There was a woman, Radhika Coomaraswamy, who had worked with Irene. She became the UN representative on the women's commission. She was a Hindu and it's quite difficult to get very far in Sri Lanka if you are not a Buddhist, so she figured that was a good way to go. She was the most helpful. That was the last of my professional trips abroad.

We also went to Norway, Switzerland, and to Italy. We stayed with Ester Boserup, who was a scholar of women in economic development. That Christmas we went to Salt Lake City and went skiing.

About five years after the Asia Democracy Program was initiated, I was asked to go back and evaluate it. There was only one center that was open and they weren't doing very much in the way of training people. I knew the guy who was the head of the program, and he was an academic, not a trainer. So there wasn't very much going on. I recommended that the program be terminated, so it was. I don't know whether this had a negative effect on my relations with USAID. There were several other occasions where they used me to either design or evaluate programs.

1994–1997

In 1994, Jack Sullivan got me a position as a tour director on a cruise ship in the South Pacific. He had been doing this himself for several years and had gotten tired of it because it was always the same trip. We picked up the ship in Singapore, from where it went to Medan (in Indonesia) and then from Medan down to Jakarta, from Jakarta to Bali. My job was, essentially, to give the passengers on the cruise ship some idea of the history and the politics of Indonesia. In most cases I went ashore with them but I was not expected to handle the 180–200 passengers since they had their own guides to take them around the cities. Irene gave some lectures on women's positions, just for fun. When we went to Bali, we stayed in the fanciest places, unlike the hotels where we stayed as students. We also got to see the Komodo dragons: these are unique because they crawl around on the ground like a crocodile with little legs. They are vegetarian and they like swampy land.

From Komodo, we went back up to the West Central Coast of Sulawesi, where they buried everybody up by the caves. Then we went from there back to Singapore. As a matter of fact, this was the last trip that this excursion ever took. It was a French line called The Paquet. Apparently, they were not doing well financially. They sold their ship and went out of business.

In 1994, we tried to sell Jambatan (Jambatan means bridge in Indonesian), our summer house in southern Maryland, right off Chesapeake Bay. We were living in Berkeley by that time and we had tried to rent it out. Somebody was going to buy it, and they went bankrupt. Eventually we gave it to the Nature Conservatory as a tax write-off, and they sold it to a couple who weatherized it. We went to see it and it had lost all its architectural charm; it was a house, not just a summer place. Later that summer we had a family reunion, three adult children but only one grandchild, Eliot, as Tjip left Hannah with her grandmother, in Russian River, north of San Francisco, for a week. The river ran too fast to swim, so we toured the wine country instead.

All this time, I was teaching part-time at Berkeley. In January 1995 we flew to Chile, where one of Irene's colleagues was studying urban gardens on his sabbatical. In June we took a trip with Tjip and Mary Beth so we could spend more time with Eliot and Hannah; we rented a house in Kentucky for a week. We drove back to Bloomington in time for Mary Beth's surprise birthday party.

I was teaching the Micropolitics of Development. When Ed Blakely was still the head, he was very helpful. Then he took off to Australia with his wife, who was from there, but wasn't happy and returned to USC. The new department head wanted to teach the courses that I was teaching. It was easy for him to take over since each semester I had to sign a contract. Then I took a year off to go around the world and teach for the Semester at Sea. I taught at Cal for six years, and then the last three years I didn't. I told him that I was willing to teach the courses free of charge. I was getting retirement payments from American University, so I didn't have to worry about getting money from UC Berkeley, which paid about $6,000 per course. But, since he was teaching the courses, he had no reason to do it. So in 1996, I stopped teaching.

In 1997 we were on the Semester at Sea. Irene was hired to teach Women in Development, and I was hired to teach

Urban Development. We flew across to the Bahamas. The boat waiting there had a capacity of approximately 650 students and about 30 faculty. Then we set off from the Bahamas. The first place we stopped was La Guaira in Venezuela. Then, I think Santiago, on the northern Atlantic coast of Brazil. We didn't go to Rio de Janeiro. From Brazil we went over to Cape Town, South Africa. Then we went to Mombasa, Kenya, and all the way to Chennai in India, and from Chennai to Ho Chi Minh City in Vietnam. From there, to Osaka in Japan and eventually we wound up in Seattle. We were supposed to contact people who could tell the students something about the problems of development administration in their cities. We found there were three classes of students on the ship. The first group took their studies very seriously and would accompany us when we interviewed various people who had something to say in our particular fields whenever we went ashore at a city. A second group went along, essentially, for the ride. Then there was the third group, who went along for tourism. Several of them had families that followed them, not on the boat, but by land or by air, and took them off to various, what would you say, exotic places in the countries we were visiting. I remember, when we were in India, for instance at Chennai, the families took their college-level kids up to places like Agra and Taj Mahal—various exotic places that really were of no interest to us because we were focusing on the problems of the cities that we went to.

CHAPTER THIRTEEN

Portland

IN 1998, TJIP WAS TEACHING AT THE UNIVERSITY OF North Carolina at Charlotte. We went to Charlotte to visit with him and, essentially, he said, "Don't ever come back [to academia]" because he was getting more and more irritated by the way he was being treated. He and Mary Beth had been in Africa on several occasions and they had promised him an Africa program. When they didn't move in that direction, he took leave to work on a USAID project in Nigeria for one year. Then USAID was so interested in what he was doing, they did a second year. The university said either you come back or resign. So USAID picked him up at that point and he is still working at USAID now.

So there we were in Berkeley. Irene had held a prominent position for nine years and decided that she would retire. But where would we go? We were interested in being near Janet and John, who were in Chicago. Our daughter Joro, who lives in Salt Lake City, wound up getting a law degree and is prominent there fighting the establishment on environmental issues. But we did not particularly want to move to Utah. Janet and John, after looking at several cities on the West Coast, decided on Portland. We were looking to retire in a place where we had children. Janet was pregnant with Owen, so we thought that it would be a good idea to be around when he was an infant. He was born right after we bought our house in Portland. We were able to see him grow up. Now he is a server at the Mirabella (where we now live). So in 1998 we bought a nice duplex up on the hill in Northwest Portland. It was a lovely location, with a beautiful view to the east. We could see Mt. Hood, Mt. St. Helens, Mt. Adams, Mt. Rainier, and Mt. Jefferson.

We were very pleased with where we were located. However, we also had Patrick, who was the neighbor from hell. When we had moved into this duplex, the only person next to us was a woman who had been working with Senator Bob Packwood. She wanted him to move in with her, but she wouldn't move in with him unless she got married to him, and he already had a house somewhere else. So they got married and they sold the duplex, and it was bought by a young couple who seemed very pleasant, both of whom had just graduated from Gonzaga University in Spokane. She was training to be a teacher and he got a job with a newspaper. But as soon as he turned twenty-one, he inherited a bunch of money from his grandma. So he quit and he started having fancy parties, and she was still trying to work. So after awhile, despite the fact that they were engaged, she moved out. Then he really started having limousines come up, and it was a dead end street. He started taking Ecstasy, we think, and he got very belligerent. He did all sorts of weird things like deciding at three in the morning to pave the street. He hired a roller and he went up and down the street at three in the morning. He had lots of friends, and people would go out, they would get it all over their feet. So he was very unpopular. At one point, he decided that it was all our fault that he was not liked on the street because we lived next to him and, therefore, we were the ones who were encouraging him to be so nasty or something.

Anyhow, he started doing all sorts of weird things to us. He had a dog and when we would go away, he would let the dog come and eat up things in our garden. We were still going back and forth to Washington, D.C., because we had this apartment out there. We still had a lot of friends in Washington and we had been visiting them, and we figured out that if we kept staying with them, they wouldn't be our friends anymore. So, we bought a small co-op apartment that was very close to the Metro and very close to downtown.

Every quarter or so, because we weren't teaching anymore, we would go stay in Washington for a month or so at a time. So we were away frequently, and every time we were away, Patrick would find some nasty thing to do. He would cut our TV connections; he would have the dog eat up our garden. He got really good at doing nasty things. The worst one was when we went away and came back, it had been raining, and these two apartments had very nice skylights on the roof. He smashed them. We had some kind of photo or something on it. We had an insurance policy that focused on what was going on, but he knew when it was going to be on and off. So he was able to bang up this skylight. There was water overhead and the water came down so when we came in, everything was soaked.

Of course we had been in touch with the police and he would never answer the door, so they could never serve him. But they knew all this history. They all knew he had done it but they couldn't prove it. But we had a good insurance policy so they came in and they ripped out everything that had been soaked. It was a mess. A lot of our books got soaked and we had to throw them out. Anyhow, after that we didn't ever leave the duplex until we moved because we were sure he'd think of something else. When we sold the duplex and decided to move into the Mirabella, the person who bought it couldn't pay the down payment. This was when all the prices tanked. So we finally decided to put our stuff in storage and go to the apartment in Washington and wait until the house sold. So the day that we finally moved out to take our stuff to storage, we parked up above our house on Cornell. His final gift to us was when we came back to it, he had thrown raw eggs all over the car. So we were rather happy to get out of there. He finally bought the house that was above so he could keep his dogs up there. But, apparently, he still is a nasty so-and-so. Nobody on the street has anything to do with him. We finally got somebody to stay up all night and serve him as he drove home. A policeman was waiting for him to come home. As he drove up, he stopped him and handed him a warrant. Multnomah County was the one that brought the case against him. Not us, not the neighborhood—but the county. During the trial, the prosecution enumerated a litany of the things that he had done so, finally, his lawyer decided to have him plead "no contest." The upshot of this is that if there was any further disturbance on that block on Pettygrove Street, they would essentially put him in prison. So the last few months had been quiet until he threw the eggs at us.

So we were kind of lured into a future at Mirabella. This building hadn't been built at the time but there were all sorts of plans and models and so forth that we were shown. We had a pretty good idea of what kind of apartments they had in the building. Before the prices sank, they had several big parties to encourage people to come and be members. You had to pay a thousand dollars to be on the list. So when we wanted to select the apartment, they had a big container of ping pong balls. They picked out the ping pong balls by your number and we didn't have a very high number. We wanted to be in this tier of apartment but at a lower level, because this was the only apartment with two bedrooms and a den. It gets more expensive every time you go up a level. We started at wanting an apartment on the tenth floor and then that was taken, and the eleventh, twelfth, thirteenth ... finally, the fifteenth. In retrospect, we are very glad about where we are.

I always said I didn't want to be that high up. A lot of the people who had reserved the apartments below us weren't able to make the down payments. So actually, eleven, twelve, thirteen, and fourteen had turned over, but we had already selected this one. We just stayed here. We also had trouble making our down payment because the people who had bought the house changed their mind. They thought with all the prices going down, everything would go down. So, what we did is when we decided to move in, I think we were about fifteen thousand dollars short from our total assets. So we went to all our kids and said, "Look, we have been giving you money all these years, we want you to give us some money back until we can get into the apartment and get our accounts stabilized." It's interesting, one of our kids immediately gave us fifteen, another said, "Well, we would have a little trouble with that, I could give you ten," and the one who has the least money gave us twenty. So, anyhow, we moved in.

We sold the place up in Portland eventually and we got a pretty good price for it. Not as much as we originally expected, but a substantial amount. The remaining amount we would acquire by selling our apartment in Washington. But it took us quite a while to sell the place in Washington because it was a co-op and there was a board and all the sales had to be approved by the board. There was one member of the board who was worried about putting the apartment up for sale because he thought that some young graduate student at George Washington University would buy it and create nuisances. It took us almost a year. Finally, the board had new elections and the one who was trying to help us get the apartment sold was re-elected, but the one who gave us the most problems was voted off the board, so we were able to sell the apartment. The people who bought it were both medical interns at GW. So it would be hard to say no to them.

CHAPTER FOURTEEN

Family Update

𝒥ANET'S SON OWEN HAS AN OLDER BROTHER, SIMON. When Owen was born, Simon must have been three or four. He was a very playful young boy and I used to spend quite a lot of time with him. He went to Grant High School and then to the University of Oregon. When he was at Grant, he was on the debate team that won the national championship. He was the chair or the captain of the team. He did very well at the University of Oregon and then went on to do graduate work. He decided to go to the University of Oregon because our daughter, Janet, works for the system and anybody who graduates with a decent score gets $5,000 off, so by the time that he finished everything, it didn't cost him very much. He wanted to save the 529 that we had put in for college for graduate school, which is exactly what he did. So he graduated quite well and then he got into Stanford for his master's degree and the 529 covered it—barely! His girlfriend Natalie moved with him and worked at various jobs.

When Simon graduated, he accepted a job up in Seattle. He won't tell us where he works. He went to work for a commercial company that is afraid that if people knew what they were working on, they would copy it. So, technically, he won't tell anybody where he works. Even his parents don't know. But he and Natalie rented a house that is within walking distance and you could figure it out but they don't bother.

Owen went to the University of Oregon for two years and his grades were okay but he felt that they didn't offer courses on what he wanted to study, so he dropped out. He is quite an accomplished artist and he wanted to be enrolled in courses that dealt with art and that use the computer for demonstration, but most of the art courses there were very traditional. So his mom said, "If you are going to live at home, you get a job." He worked for a year or so as a server at the Mirabella and enjoyed it. Most everyone knows that he is our grandson. He does art for the Mirabella magazine and had his work shown in the reception hall. He also illustrates some of Janet's programs. He was earning an income for the first time. When the coronavirus struck, he quit his job and decided to enroll at PSU and finish his degree. He has moved in with friends from UO and is considering advanced programs in computer art.

Tjip and Mary Beth's oldest is Eliot, who went to Washington University in St. Louis. He had a half scholarship, which helped because it is very expensive. He did a lot of work on campus, and he told us that he was so busy doing this work that he didn't expect to get a job offer right away. But, in fact, he got three because his field is in great demand: robotics. He went to work for Amazon in Seattle for three years and his college girlfriend Michele followed him there. When she got a job in the Bay Area, Amazon offered him a job there but he said no, he wanted to go work for something smaller. He joined the administration of Lyft. In June 2017, Eliot and Michelle Brush got married and bought a house in Oakland, where he can commute by BART. In November of 2020 they presented us with our first great-grandchild: Zoey Samantha.

Eliot's sister, Hannah, earned her master's degree from Harvard's Kennedy School studying policy. After graduation from college, she worked for two years with AmeriCorps in Minneapolis, one year as a volunteer and one year as an administrator for it. Then she decided that she needed to go to graduate school. She had been an undergraduate at Macalester College and she used up most of her 529 there, so she saved up her money and got a scholarship as well. Tjip loaned her some money to keep her from having to take out loans. She did her thesis studying New Orleans and got a job there. Her boyfriend also decided to work in Louisiana, and they are now living in Baton Rouge.

Our daughter Joro, in Salt Lake City, has one daughter, Daji (Landis), who graduated virtually in 2021 from UCLA. For her junior year in high school she got a fellowship that paid all expenses to go to Germany. She learned German and then she joined the German school speakers at UCLA. This last summer she also had a paid, all-inclusive trip to Potsdam. She graduated in math and computer sciences and is now looking into graduate school.

Editing my memoirs has made me realize that there is more to add. As I have orated my more recent memories and been asked questions about them, I have been reminded of other things that I realize I must include. I have told many friends about this project and they are interested in reading it when it is complete. However, if I try to include everything I will never finish so it will need to be work in progress.

AHM WITH IRENE AND CHILDREN VIEWING
A MOSQUE OUTSIDE NEW DELHI

MIL IN TRISHAW IN INDONESIA

AT THE SEASIDE CHALET ON THE BEACH OUTSIDE KARACHI
SHARED BY EMPLOYEES AT USAID SHOWING AHM, ADELAIDE,
OUR THREE CHILDREN AND THE DANCING MONKEY

INDEPENDENCE DAY PARADE IN NEW DELHI – KIDS
HEAD VISIBLE AT THE BOTTOM OF THE PICTURE

CHEVY CHASE HOUSE AS WE BOUGHT IT WITH FLAKING WHITEWASH

IRENE RUNS FOR THE MARYLAND HOUSE OF DELEGATES:
HEIDI AND CHILDREN HAND OUT BROCHURES

TJIP PARTICIPATING IN THE PEOPLE'S VILLAGE ON THE MALL IN DC

MIL IN FRONT OF OUR VOLVO

JANET ON STEPS OF CONGRESS PROMOTING THE ERA

JORO AND JANET ON CAPITOL STEPS DURING
DEMONSTRATIONS AGAINST THE VIETNAM WAR

GOVERNMENT BUILDING IN BANGKOK WITH MURAL
DEPICTING REVOLUTIONS WITH DATES

BALI IN FRONT OF ROOM WHERE WE STAYED AT THE
INLAND ART VILLAGE AND BOUGHT SCULPTURES

MIL INSPECTING A PROJECT IN INDONESIA

IRENE ADMIRING A WAT IN BANGKOK

MIL BEFORE A SIGN WELCOMING HIM TO PADANG

MIL PAYING A SMALL TRANSIT VEHICLE IN BANGKOK

WITH STUDENTS MIL'S TEACHING IN JOGJA AT BOROBORDUR

A SOCIAL HALL AT ST. JOHN'S UNIVERSITY. CONSTRUCTION
WAS SUPERVISED BY MY FATHER. TAKEN IN 1983.

ME ON THE STAIRCASE OF MY CHILDHOOD HOME,
NO. 9 ST. JOHN'S UNIVERSITY IN SHANGHAI

ME IN FRONT OF NO. 9 ST. JOHN'S UNIVERSITY. TAKEN IN 1983.

THE SHANGHAI AMERICAN SCHOOL. TAKEN IN 1983.

HIKING IN NEPAL WHEN ON OUR FULBRIGHT

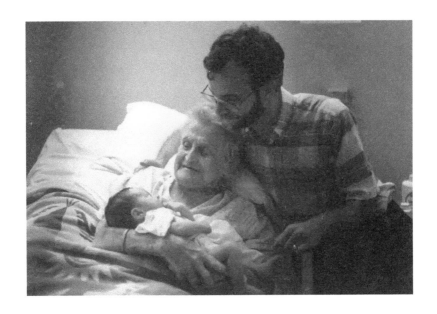

JOHN, JANET, JONO, AND PAT

JERO & NORMAN BROWN, 2002

IRENE & JANET BROWN, 2002

IN SAN JUAN'S THIS SUMMER, JULY 4, 2011
ELIOT, TJIP, MAYBETH, & HANNAH

IRENE, MIL, ALL KIDS & GRANDKIDS, 2016

PHOTO BY BOB FRENCH

CPSIA information can be obtained
at www.ICGtesting.com
Printed in the USA
JSHW040012200522
26117JS00006B/17